# At Issue

## Do Schools Prepare Students for a Global Economy?

D1502706

# Other Books in the At Issue Series:

# At Issue

## Do Schools Prepare Students for a Global Economy?

*Judeen Bartos, Book Editor*

**GREENHAVEN PRESS**
*A part of Gale, Cengage Learning*

GALE
CENGAGE Learning·

Detroit • New York • San Francisco • New Haven, Conn • Waterville, Maine • London

Elizabeth Des Chenes, *Director, Publishing Solutions*

*For more information, contact:*
Greenhaven Press
27500 Drake Rd.
Farmington Hills, MI 48331-3535
Or you can visit our Internet site at gale.cengage.com

For product information and technology assistance, contact us at

Gale Customer Support, 1-800-877-4253
For permission to use material from this text or product, submit all requests online at www.cengage.com/permissions.

Further permissions questions can be e-mailed to permissionrequest@cengage.com.

Articles in Greenhaven Press anthologies are often edited for length to meet page requirements. In addition, original titles of these works are changed to clearly present the main thesis and to explicitly indicate the author's opinion. Every effort is made to ensure that Greenhaven Press accurately reflects the original intent of the authors. Every effort has been made to trace the owners of copyrighted material.

Cover image © Todd Davidson/Illustration Works/Corbis.

**LIBRARY OF CONGRESS CATALOGING-IN-PUBLICATION DATA**

Do schools prepare students for a global economy? / Judeen Bartos, book editor.
p. cm. -- (At issue)
Summary: "Do Schools Prepare Students for a Global Economy?: Books in this anthology series focus a wide range of viewpoints onto a single controversial issue, providing in-depth discussions by leading advocates, a quick grounding in the issues, and a challenge to critical thinking skills"-- Provided by publisher.
Includes bibliographical references and index.
ISBN 978-0-7377-4094-3 (hardback) -- ISBN 978-0-7377-4095-0 (paperback)
1. Education--Economic aspects--United States. 2. Economic development--Effect of education on--United States. 3. Education--Aims and objectives--United States. 4. Education and globalization--United States. 5. Educational change--United States. I. Bartos, Judeen.
LC66.D6 2012
370.973--dc23

2012009230

Printed in the United States of America
1 2 3 4 5     16 15 14 13 12

FD195

# Contents

# Introduction

A new global situation faces the United States. The world is shrinking, and every nation confronts a future that is increasingly interconnected and interdependent. Technological and economic forces have created competition where in previous generations there was none. Against this backdrop, American schools are encountering criticism for their failure to prepare students to compete with global peers.

The Program for International Student Assessment (PISA) is an assessment administered to 15-year-olds in industrialized countries every three years, testing students' capabilities in reading, math, and science. The latest available results are from 2009 and show American students could score no higher than a 17<sup>th</sup> place finish in reading. Further, students from Shanghai, China, swept first place in all three disciplines. This, critics say, proves that American children are not prepared to compete in the global economy that awaits them.

Yong Zhao, Presidential Chair and Associate Dean for Global Education at the University of Oregon, asserts that American schools cannot afford to ignore what is going on in the rest of the world. "As institutions charged with the responsibility for preparing future citizens, schools must educate students to become competent citizens of the global village," says Zhao in a September 2009 article in the journal *Educational Leadership*. But Zhao cautions against overreacting. He maintains that US schools should not seek to imitate other countries without first recognizing America's traditional strengths— autonomy, diversity, and the ability to provide a well-rounded education to students from a variety of backgrounds. The more complex nature of America's educational system is threatened if decisions are based solely on test results.

In 2001, the US Congress enacted the No Child Left Behind Act (NCLB) in an attempt to increase academic achievement in the United States. The NCLB set high standards and measurable goals and requires that all schools and students be held accountable. While NCLB has prompted schools to place increased focus on academic results, the standardized tests used to assess progress have had unintended consequences. Since NCLB uses reading and math test scores as the primary measures of success, some schools and teachers have narrowed their focus to only material they know will be tested. This has had a detrimental effect on other academic areas such as science and social studies, and has led many schools to drop programs such as music, art, and physical education altogether in their quest to increase reading and math performance.

The pressure is high on schools to demonstrate student achievement. Schools who cannot meet NCLB goals are at risk of losing funding, and test scores have also been used to assess individual teacher performance. Critics of NCLB's use of standardized tests as the primary measure of success argue that often students who perform well on the tests are not the same ones who will succeed in an environment outside of school, where the ability to problem solve and think critically will be much more valuable than filling in answer bubbles on a multiple choice test.

There is some irony in America's drive to compete with other countries by increasing its emphasis on testing. Some observers note that many of the same countries that outperform American students on the PISA seek to emulate an American education that has consistently produced innovative, inventive students who can think for themselves after their schooling is over. Vivek Wadhwa is one such observer. In a January 2011 column in *Bloomberg/Businessweek* magazine, Wadwha, the Director of Research at the Center for Entrepreneurship and Research Commercialization at Duke University, writes "The independence and social skills American children develop give them a huge advantage when they join the workforce. They learn to experiment, challenge norms, and take risks. They can think for themselves, and they can innovate. This is why America remains the world leader in innovation; why Chinese and Indians invest their life savings to send their children to expensive U.S. schools when they can."

Indeed, as critics decry American students' ability to compete globally, examples of success can be found in schools using both old and new methods of educating students. For example, the Montessori philosophy of education was developed by Maria Montessori more than 100 years ago and endures as a proven method of providing children a well-rounded education that encourages creativity and higher-order thinking. Prominent graduates of Montessori-based schools credit their education as one of the keys to their success in later life. The co-founders of Google, Larry Page and Sergey Brin, have both said that attending a Montessori school taught them to be self-directed and self-starters. Page and Brin are not alone. Jeff Bezos, CEO of Amazon, musical entrepreneur Sean Combs, also known as P. Diddy, and chef Julia Child are other examples of Montessori graduates who have gone on to highly successful careers.

The School of One in New York City is an example of a bold new attempt to transform American schools. The School of One uses technology and up-to-date data to provide an individual education for each of its students. The pilot program has received attention as the way of the future. Arthur Levine, president of the Woodrow Wilson National Fellowship Foundation, a non-profit organization that attempts to maximize human potential through education, writes about the School of One in the *Huffington Post* in September 2009. Levine shares his enthusiasm for this innovative new model, stating "We have learned much about education since today's schools were created. We know now that what students learn and what they are taught are different, and that learning is what matters. We know that children learn different subjects at different rates, some slower and some faster. We know that children have different learning styles, which make different methods of instruction more or less effective for them. We also know that today's new technologies offer the prospect of individualizing education for each child and gearing instruction to the student's particular learning style and most effective means of instruction."

While individual examples of success such as the School of One are evident, large-scale implementation has proven elusive. The challenges of a weak American economy have made the task even more difficult. School funding at all levels has been slashed as the country struggles with its financial situation, forcing passionately debated cuts to staff and services.

One thing that all parties do agree on is that satisfaction with the status quo is not good enough in our fast-paced, ever-changing world. Educational expert Linda Darling-Hammond echoes this sentiment in the June 2010 issue of *The Nation*, stating "To meet twenty-first-century demands, the United States needs to move beyond a collection of disparate and shifting reform initiatives to a thoughtful, well-organized and well-supported set of policies that will enable young people to thrive in the new world they are entering." The viewpoints in *At Issue: Do Schools Prepare Students for a Global Economy?* reflect this and other perspectives on this important topic.

# 1

# US Student Achievement Trends Downward as Other Countries Improve

*Linda Darling-Hammond*

*Linda Darling-Hammond is professor of education at Stanford University. She is the author or editor of more than a dozen books, including* The Flat World and Education: How America's Commitment to Equity Will Determine Our Future *published in 2010.*

*Forty years ago, the United States was the undisputed world leader in education. Much has changed in the decades since, and America finds itself unable to gain traction in its efforts to educate all of its children equally. As other nations have committed to the goal of educating all citizens, children in the United States encounter vastly different educational experiences depending on their race and socioeconomic background.*

*This was not always so, as the country made significant progress in closing achievement gaps during the 1970s. Efforts since the mid-1980s, however, have been more focused on saving money, underfunding not only education but other key support systems such as health and human services. A coordinated, sustained commitment is needed to change course and raise student performance in the United States from its current status near the bottom.*

Linda Darling-Hammond, "Restoring Our Schools," *The Nation*, May 27, 2010. © 2010 by The Nation. All rights reserved. Reproduced by permission.

In 1989 President George H.W. Bush and the nation's governors convened to establish a set of six national education goals to be accomplished by the year 2000. Among these were to ensure that all students enter school healthy and ready to learn, that at least 90 percent of students graduate from high school, that all students are competent in the academic disciplines and that the United States ranks "first in the world in mathematics and science achievement."

In 2010 none of these goals have been accomplished, and we are further away from achieving most of them than we were two decades ago. More children live in poverty and lack healthcare; the high school graduation rate has slipped below 70 percent; the achievement gap between minority and white students in reading and math is larger than it was in 1988; and US performance on international tests has continued to drop.

Far from being first in the world in math and science, the United States ranked thirty-fifth out of the top forty countries in math—right between Azerbaijan and Croatia—when the most recent Programme in International Student Assessment tests were given in 2006. In science, the United States ranked twenty-ninth out of forty, sandwiched between Latvia and Lithuania. These rankings and scores had dropped from 2000, when the No Child Left Behind [NCLB] Act was introduced. While the United States performs closer to international averages in reading, its scores also dropped on the international reading tests during the NCLB era.

---

*The United States is . . . among the nations where socioeconomic background most affects student outcomes.*

---

Declines on international tests and a flattening of growth on the National Assessment of Educational Progress occurred even as state test scores used for NCLB were driven upward. This is partly because the international assessments demand more advanced analysis than do most US tests. They require students to weigh and balance evidence, apply what they know to new problems and explain and defend their answers. These higher-order skills are emphasized in other nations' curriculums and assessment systems but have been discouraged by the kind of lower-level multiple-choice testing favored by NCLB.

In addition, inequality has an enormous influence on US performance. White and Asian students score just above the average for the European OECD [Organisation for Economic Co-operation and Development] nations in each subject area, but African-American and Hispanic students score so much lower that the national average plummets to the bottom tier. The United States is also among the nations where socioeconomic background most affects student outcomes. This is because of greater income inequality and because the United States spends much more educating affluent children than poor children, with wealthy suburbs often spending twice what central cities do, and three times what poor rural areas can afford.

---

*At a time when three-quarters of the fastest-growing occupations require postsecondary education, our college participation rates have slipped from first in the world to seventeenth.*

---

Both segregation of schools and inequality in funding have increased in many states over the past two decades, leaving a growing share of African-American and Hispanic students in highly segregated apartheid schools that lack qualified teachers; up-to-date textbooks and materials; libraries, science labs and computers; and safe, adequate facilities. Thus, the poor US standing is substantially a product of unequal access to the kind of intellectually challenging learning measured on these international assessments.

During his historic campaign for the presidency, Barack Obama described our large race- and class-based achievement gaps as "morally unacceptable and economically untenable." At a time when three-quarters of the fastest-growing occupations require postsecondary education, our college participation rates have slipped from first in the world to seventeenth. While more than half of young people are becoming college graduates in many European and Asian nations, fewer than 40 percent of American young people—and fewer than 20 percent of African-American and Hispanic youth—receive a college degree.

---

*Today, at least five states spend more on corrections than they spend on public colleges or universities . . .*

---

## Failure to Invest in Education Leads to Lower Worldwide Status

In minority communities, a greater number join the growing ranks of inmates in what the *New York Times* recently dubbed our "prison nation," which incarcerates more people than any other country in the world. With 5 percent of the world's population, we have 25 percent of the world's inmates, at a cost of untold human tragedy and more than $50 billion annually to taxpayers. In an economy that requires knowledge and skills for employment and success, most inmates are high school dropouts and functionally illiterate—with literacy skills below those demanded by the labor market. States that would not spend $10,000 a year to ensure adequate education for children of color in under-resourced schools later spend more than $30,000 a year to keep them in jail.

Since the 1980s, national investments have tipped heavily toward incarceration rather than education. As the number of prisoners has quadrupled since 1980, state budgets for corrections have grown by more than 900 percent, three times faster than funds for education. With prisons and education competing for limited funds, the strong relationship between under-education, unemployment and incarceration creates a vicious cycle. Today, at least five states spend more on corrections than they spend on public colleges and universities, and some, like California, are decreasing slots in their higher education systems, as other nations are aggressively increasing theirs.

Also unlike high-achieving nations, we have failed to invest in the critical components of a high-quality education system. While we have been busy setting goals and targets for public schools and punishing the schools that fail to meet them, we have not invested in a highly trained, well-supported teaching force for all communities, as other nations have; we have not scaled up successful school designs so that they are sustained and widely available; and we have not pointed our schools at the critical higher-order thinking and performance skills needed in the twenty-first century. Some states are notable exceptions, but we have not, as a nation, undertaken the systemic reforms needed to maintain the standing we held forty years ago as the world's unquestioned educational leader.

## High Achieving Nations Make Education Their Top Priority

Other nations have been transforming their school systems to meet the new demands of today's world. They are expanding educational access to more and more of their people, and they are revising curriculums, instruction and assessments to support the more complex knowledge and skills needed in the twenty-first century. Starting in the 1980s, for example, Finland dismantled the rigid tracking system that had allocated differential access to knowledge to its young people and eliminated the state-mandated testing system that was used for this purpose, replacing them with highly trained teachers educated in newly overhauled schools of education, along with curriculums and assessments focused on problem-solving, creativity and independent learning. These changes have propelled achievement to the top of the international rankings and closed what was once a large, intractable achievement gap.

In the space of one generation, South Korea has transformed itself from a nation that educated less than a quarter of its citizens through high school to one that graduates more than 95 percent from high school and ranks third in college-educated adults, with most young people now completing postsecondary education. Egalitarian access to schools and a common curriculum, coupled with investments in well-prepared teachers, have been part of the national strategy there as well.

Similarly, starting in the 1970s, Singapore began to transform itself from a collection of fishing villages into an economic powerhouse by building an education system that would assure every student access to strong teaching, an inquiry curriculum and cutting-edge technology. In 2003, Singapore's fourth and eighth grade students scored first in the world in math and science on the Trends in International Mathematics and Science Study assessments. When children leave their tiny, spare apartments in high-rises throughout the nation, they arrive at beautiful, airy school buildings where student artwork, papers, projects and awards are displayed throughout; libraries and classrooms are well stocked; instructional technology is plentiful; and teachers are well trained and well supported.

---

*The pace at which many nations in Asia and Europe are pouring resources into forward-looking systems that educate all their citizens to much higher levels is astonishing.*

---

A visit to Nan Chiau Primary School, for example, finds fourth and fifth graders eagerly displaying the science projects they have designed and conducted in an "experience, investigate and create" cycle that is repeated throughout the year. Students are delighted to show visitors their "innovation walk," displaying student-developed projects from many subject areas lining a long corridor. Students study plants, animals and insects in the school's eco-garden; they run their own recycling center; they write and edit scripts for the Internet radio program they produce; and they use handheld computers to play games and create mathematical models that develop their quantitative abilities. Teachers, meanwhile, engage in research sponsored by the government to evaluate and continually improve their teaching.

Certainly there are schools that look like this in the United States. But they are not the norm. What distinguishes systems like Singapore's is that this quality of education—aimed at empowering students to use their knowledge in inventive ways—is replicated throughout the entire nation of 4.8 million, which is about the size of Kentucky, the median US state. Furthermore, Singapore is not alone. The pace at which many nations in Asia and Europe are pouring resources into forward-looking systems that educate all their citizens to much higher levels is astonishing. And the growing gap between the United States and these nations—particularly in our most underfunded schools—is equally dramatic.

Contrast the picture of a typical school in Singapore with the description of a California school, from a lawsuit filed recently on behalf of low-income students of color in schools like it throughout the state, a half-century after *Brown v. Board of Education*:

> At Luther Burbank, students cannot take textbooks home for homework in any core subject because their teachers have enough textbooks for use in class only. . . . For homework, students must take home photocopied pages, with no accompanying text for guidance or reference, when and if their teachers have enough paper to use to make homework copies. . . . Luther Burbank is infested with vermin and

roaches and students routinely see mice in their classrooms. One dead rodent has remained, decomposing, in a corner in the gymnasium since the beginning of the school year. . . . The school library is rarely open, has no librarian, and has not recently been updated. The latest version of the encyclopedia in the library was published in approximately 1988. . . . Luther Burbank classrooms do not have computers. Computer instruction and research skills are not, therefore, part of Luther Burbank students' regular instruction. . . . The school no longer offers any art classes for budgetary reasons. . . . Ceiling tiles are missing and cracked in the school gym, and school children are afraid to play . . . in the gym because they worry that more ceiling tiles will fall on them during their games. . . . The school has no air conditioning. On hot days classroom temperatures climb into the 90s. The school heating system does not work well. In winter, children often wear coats, hats, and gloves during class to keep warm. . . . Eleven of the 35 teachers at Luther Burbank have not yet obtained full, non-emergency teaching credentials, and 17 of the 35 teachers only began teaching at Luther Burbank this school year.

Under these kinds of circumstances, when the school lacks the rudiments needed to focus on the quality of learning and teaching or the development of higher-order thinking, it is impossible even to begin to talk about developing the deep knowledge and complex skills required of young people in today's and tomorrow's society.

---

*While nations that today are high-achieving built on the progressive reforms launched in the 1970s, the United States backpedaled in the Reagan years. . . .*

---

## Slashed Budgets Destroy Past Gains

These declines are not inevitable. We have made strong headway on educational achievement in the past and can do so again. It is easy to forget that during the years following *Brown v. Board of Education,* when desegregation and school finance reform efforts were launched, and when the Great Society's War on Poverty increased investments in poor communities, substantial gains were made in equalizing educational inputs and outcomes. Childhood poverty was reduced to levels almost half of what they are today. Investments were made in desegregation, magnet schools, community schools, pipelines of well-qualified teachers, school funding reforms and higher education assistance.

---

*We need to take the education of poor children as seriously as we take the education of the rich . . .*

---

These investments paid off in measurable ways. For a brief period in the mid-'70s, black and Hispanic students were attending college at rates comparable with whites, the only time this has happened before or since. By the mid-1970s, urban schools were spending as much as suburban schools, and paying their teachers as well; perennial teacher shortages had nearly ended; and gaps in educational attainment had closed substantially. Federally funded curriculum investments transformed teaching in many schools. Innovative schools flourished, especially in the cities. Large gains in black students' performance throughout the 1970s and early '80s cut the literacy achievement gap by nearly half in just fifteen years. Had this rate of progress continued, the achievement gap would have been closed by the beginning of the twenty-first century.

Unfortunately, that did not occur. While nations that today are high-achieving built on the progressive reforms they launched in the 1970s, the United States backpedaled in the [President Ronald] Reagan years, cutting the education budget in half, ending most aid to cities and most supports for teacher recruitment and training while also slashing health and human services budgets and shifting costs to the states. This caused states to reduce equalization aid to schools in order to pick up other social service costs.

Conservatives introduced a new theory of reform focused on outcomes rather than inputs—that is, high-stakes testing without investing—which drove most policy initiatives. The situation in many urban and rural schools deteriorated over the ensuing decades. Drops in real per-pupil expenditures accompanied tax cuts and growing enrollments. Meanwhile, student needs grew with immigration, concentrated poverty and homelessness, and growing numbers of students requiring second-language instruction and special education services. Although some federal support to high-need schools and districts was restored during the 1990s, it was not enough to recoup the earlier losses, and after 2000 inequality increased once again.

## Children's Welfare Requires Strong Investment

Although some of America's schools are among the best in the world, too many have been neglected in the more than twenty years since the clarion call for school reform was sounded in the 1980s. Clearly we need more than a new set of national goals to mobilize a dramatically more successful educational system. We also need more than pilot projects, demonstrations, innovations and other partial solutions. We need to take the education of poor children as seriously as we take the education of the rich, and we need to create systems that routinely guarantee all the elements of educational investment to all children.

What would this require? As in high- and equitably achieving nations, it would require strong investments in children's welfare—adequate healthcare, housing and food security, so that children can come to school each day ready to learn; high-quality preschool to close achievement gaps that already exist when children enter kindergarten; equitably funded schools that provide quality educators and learning materials, which are the central resources for learning; a system that ensures that teachers and leaders in every community are extremely well prepared and are supported to be effective on the job; standards, curriculums and assessments focused on twenty-first-century learning goals; and schools organized for in-depth student and teacher learning and equipped to address children's social needs, as the community schools movement has done. . . .

Thus far, [President Barack] Obama['s] administration has taken affirmative steps on a portion of this agenda. Healthcare for children has been secured in the healthcare reform bill, and investments in early childhood education have been increased, although thus far with more emphasis on expanding access than investing in high-quality teaching. The president has increased federal funding for college, which had previously dropped to a level that precluded college-going for many qualified young people who couldn't afford it.

The administration's stimulus package, which made $100 billion available for schools, has stanched some of the acute hemorrhaging of resources and staff that would otherwise have occurred last year as a result of the recession. And the president has signaled his interest in more intellectually thoughtful assessments that "don't simply measure whether students can fill in a bubble on a test but whether they possess twenty-first-century skills like problem-solving and critical thinking and entrepreneurship and creativity." This concern will be pursued through competitive grants to state consortiums that develop new assessments linked to new common core standards of learning in math and English.

The most touted aspects of the Race to the Top initiative, however, focus on peripheral issues rather than investments that have characterized major improvements in education systems at home and abroad. No nation has become high-achieving by sanctioning schools based on test-score targets and closing those that serve the neediest students without providing adequate resources and quality teaching. The implementation of Race to the Top has not required states to equalize funding to underresourced schools or even to maintain their existing commitments to these schools, many of which have had to slash budgets deeply, laying off tens of thousands of teachers, raising class size to more than forty in some cases and cutting successful programs.

In this context, schools serving high-need students are called on to raise achievement or face closure, despite evidence from the Consortium on Chicago School Research that closing more than 100 low-performing schools in that city and replacing them did not result in higher achievement.

Race to the Top requires that states expand charters but fails to assure quality and ensure access, despite evidence from the largest national study to date (conducted at Stanford University's Hoover Institution) that charter schools more frequently underperform than outperform their counterparts serving similar students; evidence from a UCLA [University of California Los Angeles] study indicating that charters exacerbate segregation; and evidence from many studies that charters serve significantly fewer special education students and English-language learners. Some excellent charters do exist, along with excellent schools run by regular public school districts, but the law does not aim to spread excellence so much as it aims to change governance. Nations that are focused on spreading quality—like Singapore, Finland and Canada, for example—have developed strategies for schools to share successful practices through networks, creating an engine for ongoing improvement for the system as a whole.

## Better Teacher Support and Preparation Is Key

Rather than establishing a framework for dramatically improving the knowledge, skills and equitable distribution of teachers, as high-achieving nations have done, Race to the Top encourages states to expand alternative routes to certification and to reduce coursework for prospective teachers, despite findings that hiring teachers from low-coursework alternatives reduces student achievement. Further, Race to the Top largely misses the critical investments needed to prepare and distribute excellent teachers and school leaders. Pay bonuses alone cannot succeed in recruiting and retaining teachers without efforts to create competitive, equitable salaries and working conditions. Removing low-performing teachers cannot improve teaching or student outcomes without strategies to ensure a stable supply of highly effective teachers who stay in their communities.

Teacher evaluation needs to become more rigorous, and rewards for effectiveness should be encouraged, but these strategies can succeed only if they are embedded in a system of universal high-quality preparation, mentoring and support—including adequately resourced and well-designed schools that allow and enable good practice. Rather than short-term incentives and quick fixes, federal policy should focus on building capacity across the entire system.

Achieving these conditions will require as much federal attention to opportunity-to-learn standards as to assessments of academic progress, and greater equalization of federal funding across states. It will require incentives for states to provide comparable funding to students, adjusted for pupil needs and costs of living, as well as incentives and information that can steer spending productively to maximize the likelihood of student success. Finally, an equitable and adequate system will need to address the supply of well-prepared educators—the most fundamental of all resources—by building an infrastructure that ensures high-quality preparation for all educators and ensures that well-trained teachers are available to all students in all communities.

While the administration's blueprint for reauthorizing the Elementary and Secondary Education Act (whose most recent iteration was No Child Left Behind) carries some hints of such strategies, its framework still envisions competition and sanctions as the primary drivers of reform rather than capacity-building and strategic investments. If this remains the primary frame for federal and state policy, it is unlikely that we will rebuild good schools in every community.

To meet twenty-first-century demands, the United States needs to move beyond a collection of disparate and shifting reform initiatives to a thoughtful, well-organized and well-supported set of policies that will enable young people to thrive in the new world they are entering. We must also finally make good on the American promise to make education available to all on equal terms, so that every member of this society can realize a productive life and contribute to the greater welfare. This is the challenge that Obama pledged to take on, and the one we should hope he will vigorously pursue.

# 2

# American Schools Possess Strengths Other Countries Want to Emulate

*Yong Zhao*

*Yong Zhao is Presidential Chair and Associate Dean for Global Education, College of Education at the University of Oregon, where he also serves as the director of the Center for Advanced Technology in Education (CATE). Zhao is the author of several publications, including* Catching Up or Leading the Way: American Education in the Age of Globalization *published in 2009.*

*The American education system is considered by many to be broken and underperforming when compared to the rest of the world. But the underlying framework of the system has traditional strengths unique to America. In the rush to match other countries' test performance, people should recognize other qualities that are not so easily measured but no less valuable—qualities such as creative thinking, innovation, independence, and entrepreneurship—at which American schools and students excel. While American policy makers try to emulate their global peers, countries such as China are at the same time abandoning some of their traditional practices in order to pursue American methods.*

Yong Zhao, "The Grass Is Greener: Learning from Other Countries," zhaolearning.com, September 18, 2011. Copyright © 2010 by Yong Zhao. All rights reserved. Reproduced by permission.

American policy makers and pundits are in love with some foreign education systems and are working hard to bring their policies and practices home. . . .

The infatuation with foreign education systems is fueled by a simple and compelling message loudly broadcast by political leaders, business tycoons, and think-tank-backed researchers: every element of American education is broken, obsolete, and in crisis, and other countries have got it all right. America's decentralized local control system has been said to be chaotic, incoherent, discriminating, and wasteful whereas others have a centralized system that ensures consistency, efficiency, and equity. American teachers are complacent, unmotivated, and ill-prepared, while teachers in other countries are of "higher cognitive ability," better prepared, and held to more rigorous accountability standards. Curriculum and textbooks in other countries are structured and well written. Students in other countries work harder. And parents in other countries care more about their children's education.

---

*Evidence suggests that the supposedly greener education pastures of other countries are largely an illusion.*

---

In short, the argument goes, to save America, to retain America's preeminence in the world, to ensure America's global competitiveness, we must dismantle America's education system and import policies and practices from other countries.

Some degree of hyperbole is understandable when a strong message needs to be sent, but the actual policy and practice proposals put forward do indeed show that America is aggressively replacing its education traditions with foreign imports. Before we complete the journey to greener pastures, it is prudent to ask a few questions that hopefully can stimulate some second thoughts about this migration.

## Fear Motivates Reform

American's love affair with education systems in other countries, ironically, stems from its fear of others. In the 1950s, the former Soviet Union scared Americans with the launch of Sputnik, the first man-made satellite, and resulted in the National Defense Education Act (NDEA). In the 1980s, the Japanese scared Americans with their automobiles and resulted in *A Nation at Risk*. In the 1990s, East Asian countries such as Singapore and South Korea scared Americans with their stellar performance in math and science in the *Third International Mathematics and Science Study* (TIMSS) and accelerated the standards movement. In the 21$^{st}$ Century, China and India began to scare Americans. Most recently, China's top ranking on the PISA [Program for International Student Assessment] was called another Sputnik moment.

It is one thing to be vigilant, to constantly and continuously evaluate and improve, and to learn from others. It is another to panic, to act out of fear, and to blindly glorify others. Evidence suggests that the supposedly greener education pastures of other countries are largely an illusion.

---

*[T]he linkage between economic growth and education is neither linear nor unidirectional.*

---

The Soviet Union, which was said to have a superior education, has now become former. Japan, which supposedly had a leading "learning gap" ahead of the U.S., has been undergoing a decade of slow growth and recently been replaced by China as the world's second largest economy. And Singapore, South Korea, Japan, and China have since the 1990s been diligent students of American education, launching reforms to emulate what America is eager to throw away.

Why?

The belief that education in certain other countries is superior has mostly started with and reinforced by a myopic

27

perspective of what constitutes high quality education. This perspective easily leads to the tendency to quickly jump to the conclusion that when a country rises economically (in the case of Japan and China) or militarily (in the case of the Soviet Union), it must have an excellent education system. The same perspective also leads to the conclusion that high test scores indicate educational excellence. As a result, observers rushed to Russia, Japan, China, Singapore, Finland, and Korea to search for their secrets to educational excellence and of course found what they wanted to find: standardized curriculum, focus on academic subjects that "matter," teachers prepared and incentivized to deliver the prescribed subjects efficiently, and well-disciplined students devoted to mastering the prescribed content, with parental support.

But the linkage between economic growth and education is neither linear nor unidirectional. Economic growth can both benefit from and benefit education. Test scores on international standardized assessment in a few subjects are not necessarily valid or accurate measures of the quality of education and are certainly not great predictors of a nation's prosperity. American students have a long history of poor performance on international assessments, always showing at the bottom since the First International Mathematics Study in the 1960's. But President [Barack] Obama said in his 2011 State of the Union speech:

> America still has the largest, most prosperous economy in the world. No workers—no workers are more productive than ours. No country has more successful companies, or grants more patents to inventors and entrepreneurs. We're the home to the world's best colleges and universities, where more students come to study than any place on Earth.

Since the poor American test takers on the First, Second, and Third international and mathematic studies have apparently not ruined America's economic and innovation records, and other high scorers have not taken over, we should seriously ask the question: is grass on the other side of the ocean really greener?

Perhaps instead of defining [as researcher Marc Tucker has] a "high-performing national education system as one in which students' achievement at the top is world class, the lowest performing students perform not much lower than their top-performing students, and the system produces these results at a cost well below the top spenders", we need to look beyond students' achievement, i.e. test scores, for qualities that are not easily measured such as independent and creative thinking, entrepreneurship, talent diversity, and emotional well-being? Measuring these qualities may show that "U.S. schools are still ahead—way ahead," as [V.] Wadhwa recently wrote in *Business Week* ([January 12,] 2011).

## Are "happy families all alike?"

Those enamored with foreign education systems seem to have taken Leo Tolstoy's opening line of *Anna Karenina* too seriously and forgotten the second part: "every unhappy family is unhappy in its own way." They attempt to extract some universal factors of the "happy families" or "high achieving education system" and apply them to the unhappy American education. For example, the recently released paper by Marc Tucker of the National Center for Education and the Economy (NCEE) tries to develop an agenda for American education reform by "standing on the shoulders of giants," that is education giants—countries with high test scores on the PISA "This paper is the answer to a question: What would the education policies and practices of the United States be if they were based on the policies and practices of the countries that now lead the world in student performance"? Earlier McKinsey and Company tried to do the same with *How the World's Best-Performing School Systems Come out on Top.*

There are at least two problems with this view. First, there are really no completely happy families all the time. The educational systems with high scores all have their own problems and challenges. The Asian systems are struggling to liberate their students from a test-driven education so they can be more creative, entrepreneurial, confident, and critical thinkers. Finland faces challenges of how to educate an increasingly culturally and ethnically diverse population and address the achievement gaps between girls and boys as well as Swedish speaking students and Finnish speaking students.

Of course, a system does not have to be perfect to offer something we can learn but then here is the second problem: "happy families" are not really alike. What works for one system does not necessarily work for others. The McKinsey report discovers the "secrets" in the "black box" that leads to success:

- The quality of an education system cannot exceed the quality of its teachers;

- The only way to improve outcome is to improve instruction;

- High performance requires every child to succeed.

Tucker's analysis of the giants resulted in a much longer list that includes clear goals and expectations, high quality teachers, high quality principals, exams and incentives for students, sorting students using external exams, access to high-quality education for all students, accountability and autonomy.

Not exactly a list of earth-shattering findings that would give me the a-hah moment. These generic abstractions disguise the real differences in policies and practices of the high-achieving systems. "There are few things that all of the most successful countries do," admits Tucker, and "[I]n fact, examples of excellent practice in almost every arena of importance can be found in the United States."

To be fair, both the Tucker and the McKinsey papers attempt to describe how these abstracted factors are differently realized in each educational context, but that is precisely my point. Not all happy families are alike, at least not in terms of what made them happy. Finland's success may come from high-quality teachers and teaching, local autonomy, and an egalitarian and homogenous society, while East Asian systems succeed from a meritocratic centralized system that places high stakes on test scores, which the Finns reject. Perhaps what is truly common across the high performers on the PISA is their small geographical size and relatively homogenous population, when compared to the United States.

What makes one happy can also be the cause of unhappiness. For instance, Finland's egalitarian approach has caused concerns about not offering enough opportunities for the gifted and talented students. Its cultural homogeneity is the source of challenges for educating culturally diverse students. And in Asia, the exclusive focus on testing scores and devotion to a few academic subjects are the sources of frustration over a lack of creativity and innovative talents. These countries are not celebrating what their students have learned, but are concerned what has been excluded. In *Strong Performers and Successful Reformers in Education: Lessons from PISA for the United States*, OECD [Organization for Economic Cooperation and Development] writes about the # 1 PISA scorer, Shanghai-China:

> Compared with other societies, young people in Shanghai may be much more immersed in learning in the broadest sense of the term. The logical conclusion is that they learn more, even though what they learn and how they learn are subjects of constant debate. Critics see young people as being "fed" learning because they are seldom left on their own to learn in a way of their choice. They have little direct encounters with nature, for example, and little experience with society either. While they have learned a lot, they may not have learned how to learn.

## What and How to Learn from Other Countries

I am not opposed to learning from other nations. In fact, I have been a strong advocate for global educational exchanges and learning from each other. But I am opposed to *handan xuebu*, a Chinese tale that tells of a young man who has no confidence in himself, even his own way of walking, and decides to go to *Handan* to imitate its style of walking but eventually forgets how to walk.

---

*We should not only look at the positive outcomes, but also the trade-offs.*

---

American education has many problems, but to paraphrase Sir Winston Churchill, is the worst form of education except for all others that have been tried. The decentralized system with local governance is a fundamentally sound framework that has evolved within the American contexts, that has led to America's economic prosperity and scientific preeminence so far, and that is being studied and copied by others. There are merits and strengths that cannot be ignored. Even today, after decades of aggressive assault and bashing, 34% of the Americans still have "A Great Deal" or "Quiet a Lot" of confidence in American public schools, with another 38% having some confidence, according to a [2011] Gallup poll. The figure is not great, but compared to the 37% in the Supreme Court, 35% in the Presidency, 19% in big business, and 12% in Congress, it definitely does not deserve to be called broken, obsolete, and have imposed upon it a complete overhaul unless such terms and actions are similarly applied to the U.S. democracy.

Thus what we can and should learn from other countries should not be attempts that destroy America's traditional strengths—a broad definition of education, a broad and well-rounded curriculum, decentralized decision making, autonomy for local communities and teachers, a philosophy that celebrates diversity, respects individual differences, and values deviation. When we learn, we should not only learn what others do, but also what others don't or do not want to do. We should not only superficially look at what policies and practices work in other countries, but also deeply examine what contextual factors (cultural, economical, societal, and traditional) made them work. We should not only look at the positive outcomes, but also the trade-offs.

In terms of how to learn, it would make much more sense and impact to engage educators, local school leaders, students, and parents in global exchanges than having governments or think-tanks to come up with what America should learn from others. A distributed global learning network of teachers, students, school leaders, and parents can truly help move education forward because these are the people who deal with concrete problems, face daily challenges, and thus know what they can borrow and what they can contribute to others. And with today's technology, the masses can engage in their global exchanges without the filtering of the so-called experts. The government just needs to grant the autonomy, creates the opportunity, and provide the support.

# 3

# US Schools Can Achieve More by Doing Less

*Lawrence Baines*

*Lawrence Baines is the chair of Instructional Leadership & Academic Curriculum at The University of Oklahoma.*

*There has been no discernible change in student achievement in the United States in over fifty years. More homework, technology, and testing along with a longer school day have not produced the desired gains. It appears that the current course the country is following may not be for the best, and corrective action is needed. Countries that are achieving at a higher level than America do not subscribe to a "more is better" approach, and American educators would do well to follow their example.*

At this moment, in school districts throughout the United States, initiatives are being launched to extend the school day, increase homework, integrate technology, and require more high-stakes testing. The assumption underlying these initiatives is that more and more—more time in school, more homework, more technology, and more high-stakes testing—will produce smarter, better-prepared students who, in turn, will help guide the nation through the tumultuous and uncertain 21st century.

To realize the ideal of an educated, productive citizenry, however, many countries around the world are employing radically different approaches. Instead of executing a strategy

Lawrence Baines, "Learning from the World: Achieving More by Doing Less," *Phi Delta Kappan*, October 2007. Reprinted with permission of Phi Delta Kappa International, www.pdkintl.org. All rights reserved.

of more and more, some countries have decided to educate their young people by doing less. Because the test scores of students from these countries routinely eclipse the scores posted by American students in two international comparisons of student achievement—Trends in International Math and Science Study (TIMSS) and Programme of International Student Achievement (PISA)—an investigation of educational practices in higher-achieving countries might prove instructive. Four areas where the policy and practice in high-achieving countries run counter to current practice and policy in the U.S. are as follows: 1) time spent at school, 2) homework, 3) technology, and 4) schools as agents of social change.

## Time Spent in School

Students in public schools in most countries in Western Europe, Canada, Mexico, Korea, Japan, and Singapore—all members of the Organisation for Economic Co-operation and Development (OECD)—spend an average of 701 hours per year in school. In Finland, where students have scored near the top in international comparisons of achievement for a number of years, students spend only 600 hours in school. In the United States, by contrast, children go to school for six or more hours per day, five days per week, for approximately 185 days spread over a period of nine or 10 months. The average time spent at school in the U.S. totals over 1,100 hours, almost double that of children in Finland. By the time children reach the age of 14 in Finland, they will have gone to school for 2,500 fewer hours than students in America (the equivalent of two to four years of schooling). Despite much longer school days, American students routinely score 10% to 20% lower than Finnish students on international tests of achievement.

Experimental studies have repeatedly found no correlation between time spent at school and levels of achievement. Of course, as any teacher in American public schools can attest, time at school is often wasted on performing nonteaching

35

tasks, organizing paperwork, maintaining discipline, and keeping students "busy." Some of the more prestigious private secondary schools in America schedule classes in the fashion of universities—90-minute periods that meet twice each week, with one day a week set aside for advising and one-on-one tutoring. If such a schedule were adopted in public high schools, for example, total instructional hours in America would drop sharply. But such a transformation would mean a departure from the traditional schedule and a retreat from the daily array of "professional development opportunities" such as hall duty, lunch supervision, bus detail, parking lot patrol, and detention hall supervision.

---

*[T]ime spent doing homework will be unconnected to academic achievement if the time is not spent productively.*

---

## Homework

As with instructional hours spent in school, America also leads the world in assigning homework—a whopping 140 minutes per week in mathematics for secondary students. Despite this extra workload, American students are renowned for posting mediocre scores on math tests. For example, the average score for an eighth-grade American student on the mathematics portion of the TIMSS in 2003 was 502. In contrast, the average Korean eighth-grader scored 584. While many Americans may suppose that Korean teachers require more from their students, in actuality, Korean teachers assign *20 minutes less homework* per week than their American counterparts. Apparently, Korean students are learning more mathematics by doing less homework.

This should not be all that surprising. As a rule, time spent doing homework will be unconnected to academic achievement if the time is not spent productively. Because most American teachers tend to assign worksheets and exercises from textbooks for homework, a student's level of engagement during the long evening hours of working at home may be less than optimal. Although much has been written about academic learning time (the time students are genuinely engaged in learning), many teachers are still more concerned with "keeping up" than with making learning interesting or relevant for their students. Obviously, as teacher salaries are increasingly tied to students' performance on tests, the urge to "cover the curriculum" to be tested is understandable. However, lack of engagement inevitably leads to apathy, frustration, and boredom.

In examining homework policies around the world, researchers have concluded, "The relationship between national patterns of homework and national achievement suggests that . . . more homework may actually undermine national achievement." Many bleary-eyed American students would wholeheartedly agree.

## Technology

A study of the integration of technology into American classrooms over the past century reveals that claims for new paths to achievement come as a matter of course with the development of new machines. In the past, some researchers have claimed academic gains associated with the use of film, radio, the tape recorder, videotape, television, and even the overhead projector. Apparently, after the novelty of a machine fades, so do claims that interactions with it will yield dramatic gains in achievement. For example, few researchers anymore would contend that an overhead projector enhances student achievement through the sheer power of its technology. Yet many schools in America have spent billions of dollars over the past 20 years under the illusion that providing students with access to computers and the Internet would somehow enhance achievement. While the universe of knowledge available via the Internet is indisputably vast, schools have been forced to restrict student access because too many websites feature pornography, ultra-violent images, or other material unsuitable for children. As a result, if they are used in schools at all, computers have taken on the role formerly occupied by a multivolume set of encyclopedias—a storehouse of concise, neatly categorized information used once or twice per year for research projects.

Undeniably, having access to the latest technologies is preferable to being relegated to a barren one-room schoolhouse with only a small, cracked chalkboard. However, technologies come with a bundle of benefits and tradeoffs. Ten years ago, the reason some high schools and universities began requiring students to come to class with laptops is that administrators believed laptops would enhance student achievement. Ten years later, the reason these same high schools and universities have stopped requiring laptops is that no evidence has surfaced to substantiate that they made any difference.

---

*Perhaps only in America could a strict regimen of standardized testing be considered an antidote to the social problems of the poor and disenfranchised.*

---

In the 2003 administration of PISA, the factor most strongly associated with high scores on reading, problem solving, and mathematics was not the presence or absence of technology, but the number of books to which a student had access. Across categories of race, gender, and nationality, the more books present in the home, the higher a student's level of achievement.

Unfortunately, in most American schools today, books are handled as if they were artifacts from a museum. Consider the following policies now enforced in many schools:

- Students are often forbidden to take books (even textbooks) home.

- If students are allowed to take books home, no more than one may be checked out of the library, and it may be checked out for only a short duration.

- Books should be used with care (students may not write in them).

School libraries, once repositories for books, have morphed into multifunctional media centers. As a result, budgets for print materials have been reduced in order to keep the computers running. Although school libraries might serve as the sole access point for books in a particular community, libraries in high-poverty urban and rural areas may have precious few books to lend. In addition, school libraries in America usually close soon after the dismissal bell, so that students, parents, and members of the community have no time to browse the shelves or simply sit down and read. Bookless homes remain bookless homes.

In most OECD countries books are not treated as artifacts but are given to students to use as they wish. They can take them home, share them, and—believe it or not—scribble notes in the margins without penalty.

## Schools as Agents of Social Change

Perhaps only in America could a strict regimen of standardized testing be considered an antidote to the social problems of the poor and disenfranchised. But No Child Left Behind gained widespread, bipartisan political support by using precisely this logic. While the federal and state governments have focused upon the establishment of school-based initiatives—setting curricular standards, specifying performance outcomes, and integrating technology—other countries have taken a broader approach to social problems. Perhaps leaders of those countries are more familiar with the research that substantiates that differences in academic achievement are more attributable to differences in social background than to variations in standardized testing.

Three dubious distinctions characterize America's poorest students: most hail from one- or no-parent households, they are the least healthy children in the country, and they score at the very bottom on achievement tests. On international achievement tests, more than one in four American students score at the lowest possible level. In Korea, only 9.6% of students score at the lowest tier; in Finland, only 6.8%.

The poverty rate in Finland is 5%, in Korea it is 15%, and in America, it is 12%. From this information, we can infer that America not only is doing an inadequate job of educating students in poverty but also is failing with significant numbers of the nonpoor. In recent decades, underachievement in America has been wholly perceived as a "school problem," and solutions have focused solely on interactions with students during school hours. The latest thinking in the United States has not been directed toward creating more family-friendly policies (such as the Canadian and European tax incentives for stay-at-home parents) or broader social initiatives, but toward putting in place more rigorous and frequent testing. A kid can try to hug a test, but the test will never hug back.

An examination of scores on standardized tests in the United States over the past 50 years reveals no discernible change in student achievement despite myriad efforts at reform. The initiatives of an extended school day, more homework, increased technology, and vigorous standardized testing, in vogue for decades, have done little to enhance achievement, promote positive attitudes, or foster good citizenship. Perhaps it is time to learn from the world, to stop thinking in terms of more and more, and consider what might be achieved by doing less.

# 4

# Low Standards Cause America's Poor Educational Performance

*Amanda Ripley*

*Amanda Ripley, a TIME Magazine contributor, is an investigative journalist who writes about human behavior and public policy. Ripley has also written for* The Atlantic, Washington Monthly, Slate, *and* New York Times Magazine.

*Stanford researcher Eric Hanushek has systematically dismantled every excuse cited to explain why American students perform more poorly than their global peers. By taking the data and breaking down the results, Hanushek disproves several common arguments, such as what he labels "the diversity excuse." The diversity excuse claims that other countries have a much more homogenous population, and that because of this they are able to outperform America, which has a higher percentage of immigrant students. But after dissecting the data down to the state level, Hanushek demonstrates that even top achieving white students fall short.*

*Massachusetts stands alone among the individual states in comparable performance with other countries. Other states would do well to copy its standards, which demand a higher level of performance from students and teachers. A lack of rigor cannot and should not be excused.*

Imagine for a moment that a rich, innovative company is looking to draft the best and brightest high-school grads from across the globe without regard to geography. Let's say this company's recruiter has a round-the-world plane ticket and just a few weeks to scout for talent. Where should he go?

Our hypothetical recruiter knows there's little sense in judging a nation like the United States by comparing it to, say, Finland. This is a big country, after all, and school quality varies dramatically from state to state. What he really wants to know is, should he visit Finland or Florida? Korea or Connecticut? Uruguay or Utah?

Stanford economist Eric Hanushek and two colleagues . . . conducted *an experiment* to answer just such questions, ranking American states and foreign countries side by side. Like our recruiter, they looked specifically at the best and brightest in each place—the kids most likely to get good jobs in the future—using scores on standardized math tests as a proxy for educational achievement.

We've known for some time how this story ends nationwide: only 6 percent of U.S. students perform at the advanced-proficiency level in math, a share that lags behind kids in some 30 other countries, from the United Kingdom to Taiwan. But what happens when we break down the results? Do any individual U.S. states wind up near the top?

---

*More money does not tend to lead to better results; smaller class sizes do not tend to improve learning.*

---

## Individual States Still Fail to Measure Up

Incredibly, no. Even if we treat each state as its own country, not a single one makes it into the top dozen contenders on the list. The best performer is Massachusetts, ringing in at No. 17. Minnesota also makes it into the upper-middle tier, followed by Vermont, New Jersey, and Washington. And down it goes from there, all the way to Mississippi, whose students—by this measure at least—might as well be attending school in Thailand or Serbia.

Hanushek, who grew up outside Cleveland and graduated from the Air Force Academy in 1965, has the gentle voice and manner of Mr. Rogers, but he has spent the past 40 years calmly butchering conventional wisdom on education. In study after study, he has demonstrated that our assumptions about what works are almost always wrong. More money does *not* tend to lead to better results; smaller class sizes do *not* tend to improve learning. "Historically," he says, "reporters call me [when] the editor asks, 'What is the other side of this story?'"

Over the years, as Hanushek has focused more on international comparisons, he has heard a variety of theories as to why U.S. students underperform so egregiously. When he started, the prevailing excuse was that the testing wasn't fair. Other countries were testing a more select group of students, while we were testing everyone. That is no longer true: due to better sampling techniques and other countries' decisions to educate more of their citizens, we're now generally comparing apples to apples.

These days, the theory Hanushek hears most often is what we might call the diversity excuse. When he runs into his neighbors at Palo Alto coffee shops, they lament the condition of public schools overall, but are quick to exempt the schools their own kids attend. "In the litany of excuses, one explanation is always, 'We're a very heterogeneous society—all these immigrants are dragging us down. But *our* kids are doing fine,'" Hanushek says. This latest study was designed, in part, to test the diversity excuse.

To do this, Hanushek, along with Paul Peterson at Harvard and Ludger Woessmann at the University of Munich, looked at the American kids performing at the top of the charts on an international math test. (Math tests are easier to normalize across countries, regardless of language barriers; and math skills tend to better predict future earnings than other skills taught in high school.) Then, to get state-by-state data, they correlated the results of that international test with the results of the National Assessment of Educational Progress exam, which is given to a much larger sample in the U.S. and can be used to draw statewide conclusions.

The international test Hanushek used for this study—the Programme for International Student Assessment, or PISA—is administered every three years to 15-year-olds in about 60 countries. Some experts love this test; others, like Tom Loveless at the Brookings Institution, criticize it as a poor judge of what schools are teaching. But despite his concerns about PISA, Loveless, who has read an advance version of Hanushek's study, agrees with its primary conclusion. "The United States does not do a good job of educating kids at the top," he says. "There's a long-standing attitude that, 'Well, smart kids can make it on their own. And after all, they're doing well. So why worry about them?'"

---

*On a percentage basis, New York state has fewer high performers among white kids than Poland has among kids overall.*

---

Of course, the fact that no U.S. state does very well compared with other rich nations does not necessarily disprove the diversity excuse: parents in Palo Alto could reasonably infer that California's poor ranking (in the bottom third, just above Portugal and below Italy) is a function of the state's large population of poor and/or immigrant children, and does not reflect their own kids' relatively well-off circumstances.

So Hanushek and his co-authors sliced the data more thinly still. They couldn't control for income, since students don't report their parents' salaries when they take these tests; but they could use reliable proxies. How would our states do if we looked just at the white kids performing at high levels—

kids who are not, generally speaking, subject to language barriers or racial discrimination? Or if we looked just at kids with at least one college-educated parent?

As it turned out, even these relatively privileged students do not compete favorably with average students in other well-off countries. On a percentage basis, New York state has fewer high performers among white kids than Poland has among kids overall. In Illinois, the percentage of kids with a college-educated parent who are highly skilled at math is lower than the percentage of such kids among *all* students in Iceland, France, Estonia, and Sweden.

Parents in Palo Alto will always insist that their kids are the exception, of course. And researchers cannot compare small cities and towns around the globe—not yet, anyway. But Hanushek thinks the study significantly undercuts the diversity excuse. "People will find it quite shocking," he says, "that even our most-advantaged students are not all that competitive."

## Massachusetts Demonstrates How to Get Results

Reading the list, one cannot help but thank God for Massachusetts, which offers the United States some shred of national dignity—a result echoed in other international tests. "If all American fourth- and eighth-grade kids did as well in math and science as they do in Massachusetts," writes the veteran education author Karin Chenoweth in her 2009 book. *How It's Being Done*, "we still wouldn't be in Singapore's league but we'd be giving Japan and Chinese Taipei a run for their money."

Is it because Massachusetts is so white? Or so immigrant-free? Or so rich? Not quite. Massachusetts is indeed slightly whiter and slightly better-off than the U.S. average. But in the late 1990s, it nonetheless lagged behind similar states—such as Connecticut and Maine—in nationwide tests of fourth- and eighth-graders. It was only after a decade of educational reforms that Massachusetts began to rank first in the nation.

What did Massachusetts do? Well, nothing that many countries (and industries) didn't do a long time ago. For example, Massachusetts made it harder to become a teacher, requiring newcomers to pass a basic literacy test before entering the classroom.

(In the first year, more than a third of the new teachers failed the test.) The state also required students to pass a test before graduating from high school—a notion so heretical that it led to protests in which students burned state superintendent David Driscoll in effigy. To help tutor the kids who failed, the state moved money around to the places where it was needed most. "We had a system of standards and held people to it—adults and students," Driscoll says.

Massachusetts, in other words, began demanding meaningful outcomes from everyone in the school building. Obvious though it may seem, it's an idea that remains sacrilegious in many U.S. schools, despite the clumsy advances of No Child Left Behind. Instead, we still fixate on inputs—such as how much money we are pouring into the system or how small our class sizes are—and wind up with little to show for it. Since the early 1970s, we've doubled the amount of money we spend per pupil nationwide, but our high-schoolers' reading and math scores have barely budged.

*Our future middle-school math teachers knew about as much math as their peers in Thailand and Oman—and nowhere near what future teachers in Taiwan and Singapore knew.*

Per student, we now spend more than all but three other countries—Luxembourg, Switzerland, and Norway—on elementary and secondary education. And the list of countries that spend the most, notably, has little in common with the outcomes that Hanushek and his colleagues put into rank order. (The same holds true on the state level, where New York, one of the highest-spending states—it topped the list at $17,000 per pupil in 2008—still comes in behind 15 other states and 30 countries on Hanushek's list.)

However haltingly, more states are finally beginning to follow the lead of Massachusetts. At least 35 states and the District of Columbia agreed this year to adopt common standards for what kids should know in math and language arts—standards informed in part by what kids in top-performing countries are learning. Still, all of the states, Massachusetts included, have a long way to go. Last year, a study comparing standardized math tests given to third-graders in Massachusetts and Hong Kong found embarrassing disparities. Even at that early age, kids in Hong Kong were being asked more-demanding questions that required more-complex responses.

Meanwhile, a 2010 study of teacher-prep programs in 16 countries found a striking correlation between how well students did on international exams and how their future teachers performed on a math test. In the U.S., researchers tested nearly 3,300 teachers-to-be in 39 states. The results? Our future middle-school math teachers knew about as much math as their peers in Thailand and Oman—and nowhere near what future teachers in Taiwan and Singapore knew. Moreover, the results showed dramatic variation depending on the teacher-training program. Perhaps this should not be surprising: teachers cannot teach what they do not know, and to date, most have not been required to know very much math.

Early last year [2009], President Obama reminded Congress, "The countries that out-teach us today will out-compete us tomorrow." This September [2010], Ontario Premier Dalton McGuinty, visiting a local school on the first day of classes, mentioned Obama's warning and smugly took note of the scoreboard: "Well," he said, "we are out-teaching them today."

Arne Duncan, Obama's education secretary, responded to the premier's trash-talking a few days later. "When I played professional basketball in Australia, that's the type of quote the coach would post on the bulletin board in the locker room," he declared during a speech in Toronto. And then his rejoinder came to a crashing halt. "In all seriousness," Duncan confessed, "Premier McGuinty spoke the truth."

# 5

# Blending Traditional and Online Learning Improves Achievement

*Jonathan Schorr and Deborah McGriff*

*Jonathan Schorr is a partner in the San Francisco office of the NewSchools Venture fund. Prior to joining NewSchools, Jonathan served as director of new initiatives at the KIPP (Knowledge is Power Program) Foundation, a network of high-performing urban public schools. Deborah McGriff is also a partner at New-Schools Venture Fund, where she works on investment strategy and quality teaching. Deborah is president of the Education Industry Association, an association of providers of educational service.*

*Hybrid schools across the nation are blending face-to-face and online learning to achieve impressive early results. The blend of human interaction and powerful technology is a model that differs from earlier efforts to bring technology into the classroom. Rather than layered on top of the existing curriculum, the online learning component is used to tailor lessons to individual students resulting in notable growth even among students in high-poverty schools where significant gains are often most difficult to attain.*

*In an era of decreased school funding, hybrid schools have also proven to be cost effective. The combination is powerful in*

Jonathan Schorr and Deborah McGriff, "Future Schools: Blending Face-to-Face and Online Learning," *Education Next*, Summer 2011. www.educationnext.com. Copyright © 2011 by The Hoover Institution. All rights reserved. Reproduced by permission.

*making a real difference in the future of students and their ability to compete in a global economy.*

The way the 1st graders hurtle toward their computer workstations, you'd think they were headed out to recess.

It's an unseasonably warm winter morning in San Jose, California, and the two dozen students at Rocketship Mateo Sheedy Elementary School get situated quickly in the computer lab, donning headphones and peering into monitors displaying their names. The kindergartners follow a moment later, until 43 seats are filled. The effect is of a miniature, and improbably enthusiastic, call center.

---

*[T]echnology will integrate with, and change, the structure of the school.*

---

This lab—and the larger plan for the school surrounding it—has probably done more than any other single place to create enthusiam for "hybrid schools." Such schools combine "face-to-face" education in a specific place (what used to be called "school") with online instruction. (Rocketship uses the term "hybrid," rather than the increasingly prevalent term "blended learning," because the computers are not actually "blended" with face-to-face instruction in the same classroom.) It's a sign of how young the hybrid and blended field is that this school at the epicenter hails all the way back to 2007. Rocketship Education, a small but burgeoning network of charter schools that serves an overwhelmingly low-income immigrant community in San Jose, has made a name through its, forgive the phrase, high-flying student performance. Two of its three schools are old enough to have test scores. They rank among the 15 top-performing high-poverty schools statewide, and the site that opened in 2009 was the number-one first-year school in the state in the high-poverty category. But what positions Rocketship on the cutting edge of school reform is its vision for how technology will integrate with, and change, the structure of the school. (Disclosure: Our firm, NewSchools Venture Fund, is a significant investor in the work of Rocketship and of several other organizations mentioned in this article.)

## Integrating Technology with Classroom Practice

The scene in the computer lab represents the first steps toward realizing the Rocketship vision. In the lab, the 1st graders log in by selecting from a group of images that acts as a personal password, and then race through a short assessment that covers math and reading problems. Faced with the prompt "Put all the striped balls in one basket and all the polka-dotted balls in the other basket," a student named Jazmine uses her mouse to move the objects to their places. Then it's on to the core activity of her 90 minutes in the lab: a lesson on counting and grouping using software from DreamBox. The scenarios are slightly surreal—more objects to move, in this case mostly fruit, and the reward for getting it right involves an animated monkey bringing yet more fruit to a stash on her island—but she and most other students take on the task assiduously. It may be a lesson, but that's not how Jazmine sees it. "This game is really easy," she says. A bit later, she'll read a book from a box targeted at her exact reading level, and make a return visit to the computer to take a short quiz about what she read.

Despite the kids' engagement in the online lesson, no one is claiming that time in front of the computer is directly responsible for the extraordinary performance of Rocketship students. Rather, the online work is essential to the long-term vision for the school's instructional model—and for Rocketship's growth trajectory. Crucially, the lab requires an adult who has experience with children, but no teaching credential (nor, indeed, bachelor's degree) is required. For this class, it's a young mother named Coral De Dios, who dispenses help and order as the moment requires. Her ability to monitor the 43 kids here means that the school requires less staff, ultimately saving hundreds of thousands of dollars each year that can be plowed back into resources for the school, including staff salaries. In cash-strapped California, that's no small matter.

But the larger impact of the technology is still ahead, in the ways it will integrate with, and alter, classroom practice. Rocketship is building a model in which kids learn much of their basic skills via adaptive technology like the DreamBox software, leaving classroom teachers free to focus on critical-thinking instruction and extra help where kids are struggling. Likewise, teachers will be able to "prescribe" online attention to specific skills. Part of the model involves providing teachers with a steady stream of data that will help them adjust instruction to kids' specific needs, and to guide afterschool tutors. Today, those linkages between the computer lab and the classroom remain incomplete, in part because the data from various online systems aren't sufficiently standardized; the many data points from different systems could be overwhelming to teachers.

Rocketship's data guru, Charlie Bufalino, says that to date, vendors haven't invested sufficiently in the R&D and technical fixes that would make a standardized stream of data possible and take menial tasks like attendance out of teachers' hands. As more schools like Rocketship build hybrid and blended systems, however, and as more entrepreneurs develop the missing-piece systems, the tipping point may be reached, fueling rapid growth of this new approach to schooling.

Rocketship and the other school models we describe here offer a vision for what deeply integrated technology can mean for children's education, for the way schools are structured, and for the promise of greater efficiency amid a lengthy economic downturn. This is much more than simply taking a class online. Already, millions of children take one or more online courses, ranging from credit recovery to Advanced Placement. And there's a wide range of ways that the school facility and online learning—"bricks and clicks"—mix. Our interest is specifically in schools and platforms that use technology intensively and thoughtfully to tailor instruction to individual students' needs, and provide robust, frequent data on their performance. Most of our examples are high-performing charter schools, which have become a particular hotbed for the type of hybrid and blended models we are describing. Their designs call for bringing new productivity to the way schools deploy staff and dollars. They all share an ambition to prepare their students for success not just on tests, but in college.

## School of One

Much of the enthusiasm for the potential of blended learning comes from what is currently a math program. School of One, operating inside three New York City public middle schools, is an exciting experiment interweaving a wide range of online learning possibilities with classroom instruction. Indeed, a visitor needs only to walk into School of One's classroom space at Intermediate School 228 in Brooklyn to see what customized education looks like. The classroom is an open space that runs the length of the building wing, but is subdivided by bookshelves into workspaces where small groups of students work with the teacher or individually with laptops. The first sight that greets the eye is an airport-style video display, listing not cities and flights, but students' names and how they will receive their instruction during that period. For those who are starting on the computer, a press of a button will take them to a lesson provided by 1 of more than 50 content providers. Each lesson runs about half an hour, and students may switch from one content provider to another on the same skill. Others work in small groups with a teacher, who will typically oversee two or three groups of students, the content and groupings informed by data from the student's work online.

---

*It's a model that seems certain to make us question assumptions about how we organize classrooms and schools.*

---

"You understand way better," says Edwin, a 12-year-old 7th grader clad in basketball-ready dark blue T-shirt, shorts, and athletic shoes. Thanks to the unusual structure of math classes at School of One, he says, teachers work with only 9 or 10 students at one time, while at other schools, "the teacher doesn't have time to go over things with every student." He adds, "It's a really good program for kids who have trouble with math."

Behind the flashy images on the laptop screens, the real power behind School of One is in its brawny "back end" systems, which enable the creation of real-time, hourly reports of students' progress and shortfalls. Teachers review these reports daily, both individually and in a collaborative planning period when they discuss the progress of individual students as well as student groups. Teachers can review the information before school, after school, during their prep period, or even while they are overseeing instruction (so they can identify the students in a group who, according to previous assessment data, may be struggling to learn a skill). "We get data every single day to help us understand what's working and what's not," says founder Joel Rose. When a student struggles on Tuesday, she can be assigned to a small group for help from a teacher on Wednesday, and with enough data and enough flexibility, it will even be possible to assign her to a teacher who is particularly good at teaching that lesson. It's a model that seems certain to make us question assumptions about how we organize classrooms and schools.

Like the teachers, students can see a map of their accomplishments. That map is tied to state standards and will later align with the Common Core standards. As at Rocketship, aligning lessons to these standards is no small matter; School of One had veteran math teachers codify the precursors and dependencies for each skill. They sourced more than 25,000 lessons for middle-school math, from which they chose the top 5,000. Many lessons were not included because they did not closely align to their map. School of One has enough faith in the power of its standards and assessments that it will soon offer students the option to press a "prove it" button that allows them to demonstrate mastery at an upcoming task and, if successful, skip it. The button stands as a testament to a core notion of the blended idea: learning that proceeds at a pace the student is ready for, rather than one set by the needs of an entire class.

---

*The data enable teachers to differentiate instruction and connect instructional strategies with student results.*

---

## DSST Public Schools

The constant, real-time stream of student assessment data is a crucial element of the most promising tech-enabled schools, including some high flyers that don't fit neatly under the blended label. One of the most interesting is charter school network DSST Public Schools, named for its flagship, the Denver School of Science and Technology. DSST enrolls a mostly-minority, 47 percent low-income student population and has achieved national renown for its extraordinary results, including the second-highest longitudinal growth rate in student test scores statewide. Among graduates, 100 percent have been accepted to four-year colleges, where an astonishing 1 percent require remedial courses, in comparison to 56 percent for the Denver district. Technology is everywhere as one strolls through DSST's Stapleton campus in northeast Denver, just barely within sight of peaks of the Front Range of the Rocky Mountains. In a 6th-grade social studies class recently, students used collaborative user-made web sites called wikis to access and respond to in-class and homework assignments. The teacher projected a map of Asia and posted prompts on the wiki for students to respond to as they learned about the geography of the region.

DSST's assessment system provides real-time, instant feedback to teachers and students on students' progress, measured through quick assessments that students take on netbooks. Teachers at DSST have been developing these informal assessments and in the 2010–11 school year are working with a consultant to review the validity of the assessment items and gather feedback that will in turn make teachers better item writers. The data enable teachers to differentiate instruction and connect instructional strategies with student results. As at School of One, both teachers and students at DSST can track mastery on a particular standard. Teachers can quickly adjust groups and/or identify topics for re-teaching. Through these assessments and classroom observations, teachers identify students in need of extra support, who are then assigned to after-school tutoring the same day. Teachers use the information to plan lessons, deciding whether to spend more class time on a certain area or focus on individual tutoring based on class scores. DSST is also using data to analyze teacher performance. "The technology enables us to collect good data on our school performance, which is used to drive and motivate student achievement," says founder and CEO Bill Kurtz. "We believe that education innovation will be driven by common data."

## Carpe Diem Collegiate High School

Elsewhere in the charter universe, schools are incorporating hybrid and blended structures into already successful school organizations, which increasingly seek efficiency, even as they expand and work to maintain excellent student achievement.

The impact has been dramatic, for example, at Carpe Diem Collegiate High School of Yuma, Arizona. Carpe Diem represents what will likely be a crucial chapter in the story of blended schools: a turn to a blended model because of financial or facilities challenges. The charter school, which serves 250 mostly low-income students in 6th through 12th grades, faced a crisis after losing its lease on a church building. Its founders radically transformed it from a traditional structure to one heavily dependent on online instruction, and in 2006 completed a facility tailored to the new model. In the reinvented school, small groups take classes directly from teachers, while most students take online classes in a learning center that features 300 low-sided cubicles in one brightly painted room. Student cubicles have a desktop computer and monitor; many have been personalized and decorated with artwork. The learning center is staffed by the principal, two instructional assistants, and a course manager, who also talks with students about their progress.

---

*Mixed-media art hangs from every wall, door, and metal roof beam, and gee-whiz technology is everywhere.*

---

Students begin their day by logging onto a software system called e2020 and accessing the calendar, selecting a subject area, and looking at their lists of assignments for the week. On any given day, based on the data, teachers may gather an entire grade or a subset of students, sometimes in groups as small as one or two. Some students work through all subjects each day, while others focus on math for the week on one day, science for the week on another day. Carpe Diem has been a state leader in student growth for the past two years.

## High Tech High

Yet, even in schools that have been aggressive in incorporating technology, there is such a thing as too much in adopting blended approaches. Such is the case at High Tech High, whose campus near the San Diego airport is perhaps the most eye-poppingly technology-rich in the country. Rooms within the warehouse-sized buildings are delineated with glass walls 15 feet high, leaving the remaining space under the 25-foot ceilings for a chaotic crisscross of air ducts, structural supports, and wires. Mixed-media art hangs from every wall, door, and metal roof beam, and gee-whiz technology is everywhere. Students use the same computer-aided design systems that they would find in a professional design firm as they model real-life, design-forward chairs. The hallways are lined by prize-winning robotics projects. And outside, students further their studies of air pressure by racing hovercraft they have designed using large circles of plywood with plastic-bag cushion edges and leaf-blower engines.

High Tech High has taken gentle steps into blended territory through its use of ALEKS [Assessment and LEarning in Knowledge Spaces], which bills itself as "a Web-based, artificially intelligent assessment and learning system." ALEKS, which runs on computers on the periphery of a 9th-grade classroom, provides teachers with detailed diagnostics, helping them to focus on the areas where students are struggling, and lets students take lessons at their own pace. A student logs on to ALEKS and begins by taking an adaptive assessment, each question chosen on the basis of previous answers. With this information, ALEKS develops a snapshot of a student's knowledge in a given content area, recognizing which topics he has mastered and which he has not. This information is represented for both the student and teacher by a multicolored pie chart, which is constantly being updated as the student masters new topics. Once a student has mastered a specific topic, new ones become available for the student to choose from. "It doesn't slow you down," says Danie, a 15-year-old boy with a dark mop of hair that he regularly brushes off his forehead. Danie, wearing untied high-tops and faded black jeans, confesses matter-of-factly that he is repeating the 9th grade. "Students learn at different speeds," he says with marked confidence. He hastens to add that the technology augments, rather than replaces, the teacher. "Nothing," he says, "can replace human interaction." Danie's teacher, Jane Armstrong, agrees, saying ALEKS gives her more flexibility in grouping students. Today, Armstrong has divided the class in two. Half of the students are using ALEKS while Armstrong is working with the other half in small groups. "This setting allows me to get to know all of my students," she says. "If I'm just lecturing them, I don't get to know what they've mastered."

California's budget situation today is nothing short of disastrous. Yet High Tech High recently rejected a much more aggressive move into the blended field, a "flex" plan that would have brought students to campus only once a week, with the other four days spent online, typically from home. The plan would have created enormous cost savings by allowing five different cohorts of students to use one building each week. Yet teachers, students, and parents rejected the idea of giving up the daily campus experience, and teachers were not enthusiastic about doing a large proportion of their teaching online. "We're not drinking the Kool-Aid," said founder and CEO Larry Rosenstock.

---

*In the past, technology actually made schooling* more *expensive, as computers were layered onto an existing model without adding any efficiency.*

---

## Financial Hard Times Fuel More Productive Learning

Indeed, it seems likely that, just as happened with charter management organizations, rapid growth will take place only when the pioneers can demonstrate proof points of excellence in student performance. "In order for there to be larger market traction, the overall industry has to see more results," says

Anthony Kim of Education Elements, a nascent firm that designs the technical back end for blended schools. "We're at the very early adopter stage right now."

Blended schooling is dawning at a time when, as recent public opinion polls show, people are open to online learning. According to the 2010 EdNext-PEPG Survey, support for online coursework jumped 8 to 10 percent in a single year. Yet as much as anything, the blended effort is being driven by a new fiscal reality. In a widely regarded speech at the American Enterprise Institute called "The New Normal: Doing More with Less," education secretary Arne Duncan noted that a loss of housing valuation meant that education funds are down sharply and aren't coming back anytime soon. In the spirit of never wasting a crisis, he said he hoped the difficult financial straits would help bring an end to "the factory model of education" and an increase in productivity in schools. He said, "Our schools must prepare all students for college and careers—and do far more to personalize instruction and employ the smart use of technology."

Is the blended school the model he's looking for? Tom Vander Ark, a former head of education for the Bill & Melinda Gates Foundation and now a partner in a private equity fund focused on education innovation, thinks so. In the past, technology actually made schooling *more* expensive, as computers were layered onto an existing model without adding any efficiency. Technology-driven productivity, he says, stands to change that. "We can make learning far more productive," says Vander Ark. "It's the first chance in history to change the curve."

# 6

# Private Funders Struggle to Make an Impact on Education Reform

*Helen Zelon*

*Helen Zelon lives in Brooklyn, New York, and is a contributing editor for* City Limits, *a project of the Community Service Society of New York.*

*Despite increased education reform funding from philanthropic foundations, systemic change has been difficult to achieve. Successful efforts have not been able to be replicated on a larger scale.*

*Foundation money represents a small percentage of total school funding, but a higher proportion of this money is directed to innovation and reform programs. While smaller in amount, private funding groups strive to sponsor projects that will result in fundamental changes in how we educate our children with the goal of promoting a healthy future for the country.*

Bill Gates is only one of several individual philanthropists who've been joined by major foundations in bankrolling school reform efforts.

Two months ago [July, 2011], Bill Gates told the *Wall Street Journal* [*WSJ*] that private money—including upwards of $5 billion in Gates foundation funding—"didn't move the needle much," in terms of substantial, measurable improvements in student achievement and graduation outcomes.

"It's hard to improve public education—that's clear," Gates said. "If you're picking stocks, you wouldn't pick this one."

Today Melinda Gates and Mr. and Mrs. Warren Buffett are talking education reform with NBC's *Education Nation*. With Gates' *WSJ* comments in mind, *City Limits* asked foundations and groups they fund: Do private dollars make a difference in public education?

The answer: Mixed.

We approached top education-reform funders like Gates, Ford, Carnegie and the Broad Foundation. We reached out to New Visions—a veteran school-management organization that's been part of developing scores of New York City schools—and to the Wallace Foundation, as well as the Annenberg Institute for School Reform.

Some foundations chose not to talk with *City Limits*; representatives of the Carnegie Foundation, for example, said that a conversation wasn't in the foundation's best interests—a no-comment that pinpoints the public-private conflict: Private foundations must protect themselves, despite their mandate to do public good. But those who spoke on the record told of reform efforts that signal potential success but face considerable challenges in scale, design and execution.

---

*Do private dollars make a difference in public education? The answer: mixed.*

---

## Individual Successes in a Big Universe

It's hardly news that some of the country's wealthiest individuals and foundations have taken up education reform as a funding project: Corporate heavyweights like Goldman Sachs are backing new efforts by the Harlem Children's Zone. Current and former hedge funders like Whitney Tilson (T2 Partners), Paul Tudor Jones II (founder of the Robin Hood Foundation) and Julian Robertson (founder of the charter-supporting Tiger Foundation) are passionately active in education reform circles. A generation of prominent, generous education reformers, also described as "venture philanthropists", have remade the education reform landscape here in New York City.

Across the board, foundations and their recipients, like the Annenberg Institute for School Reform and the New York City Department of Education, say that individual successes deserve recognition.

"We are tremendously grateful for the philanthropic support and commitment from the Gates Foundation to improving student achievement and graduation outcomes in New York City," said Department of Education [DOE] spokesperson Deidrea Miller. DOE declined to respond to specific questions about where private moneys are best invested or the effect of private investment on public policy and public education. (A staffer there told *City Limits*, "We don't really have opinions on things. Things are what they are.")

---

*Scaling up individual successes to systemic solutions has been reform's biggest challenge.*

---

But those who do elaborate say that systemic change has been harder to attain than good results in a given school.

"We have had more success on the individual-school-innovation side," Walter Simmons, executive director of the Annenberg Institute, said, citing a handful of New York City schools that blend academic and social/emotional support to keep students engaged, connected and motivated to learn. "But we haven't had that kind of success on the organizational learning and improvement side, on the systems or districts—we haven't learned from successful schools. That's the biggest challenge."

"We've been frustrated in our inability to fund and redesign systems rather than individual schools," Simmons added.

## The Price of Money

Scaling up individual successes to systemic solutions has been reform's biggest challenge.

One obvious issue is the amount of money involved. Lucas Held of the Wallace Foundation echoed Gates' observation that private money is a tiny drop in the public-education bucket: "Contributions to public education are less than 1 percent of the annual spend," Held said, referring to the $600 billion the U.S. spends every year on education. (For context, NYC's Department of Education 2011 budget was nearly $23 billion.) The Wallace Foundation targets "overlooked issues, the issues people agree are important but too costly for a single district to figure out a solution," issues like strengthening school leadership and extending summer learning to shore up student achievement, Held said.

And the amount of money dictates how it is used. Annenberg's Simmons said that less than 2 percent of the $600 billion education pot goes to promoting innovation—compared with about 10 percent innovation-investment in corporations. The resulting thin, shallow investments mean that "school systems focus on outcomes. They under-invest in understanding who students are and the communities they come from. They don't focus on their students' unique set of experiences and aspirations," or build the kind of community and mentoring partnerships that give high-need urban kids the active support to stay engaged in school. "Pockets of excellence don't scale up," he added.

## A Game with Different Rules

Both Wallace and Annenberg look to "scale up" successful reform from the individual-school level to entire districts and school systems. The Broad (rhymes with 'road') Foundation takes a systems approach: They aim to seed school districts nationwide with graduates of Broad's Principals Academy, and they reward urban districts that make outstanding progress with annual, million-dollar prizes to showcase and promote "best practices," according to Broad spokesperson Erica Lippert.

---

*[T]he economic tango between private givers and public school systems can be challenging.*

---

There's no denying the appeal of school reform to funders: "Giving back to the country, leaving an indelible imprint on society and the nation—you can have an imprint on the health of the world," Lippert said.

But while the interest in school reform is a descendent of earlier waves of philanthropy that, say, built hospitals, a critical difference separates medical research, another Broad funding area, and education reform: "The medical field uses very high, rigorous standards," Lippert said. "The National Institutes of Health sets standards, everyone's on the same page about what works. You don't have the equivalent of that in the education space. There's such a debate of what's working and what's not, it's difficult to make way through that morass."

## Partnerships Are Healthy Despite Challenges

Supporters and critics debate the virtues and weaknesses of individual efforts, but no one denies that there's a healthy cross-pollination occurring across foundation and nonprofit funders and the public entities they seek to support—a feedback loop among education reform, edu-philanthropy and elected and school-district leaders that shapes the national debate on what's best for public schools.

But the economic tango between private givers and public school systems can be challenging.

Disparate resources among city schools—a product of philanthropic funding structures that favor high-poverty schools, high-need students, schools in transition, or those

65

with robust corporate support or deep-pocketed parents to draw from—undermines the ideal of equity for all, Simmons said. "If we're expecting to close the achievement gap across the system, across the board, someone has to be thinking of equal distribution of resources with equal intensity as they apply to innovation in school reform."

Policy, practice and funding are inevitably related, says the Wallace Foundation's Held—a practical truth that's even more critical in an economically strapped time, when funds applied must be made to work. "It's certainly the case that foundations are generally looking for organizations or districts that are already moving in the direction that the [foundation] grant supports," Held said "There's a pragmatic reason for that—the grant is more likely to succeed if it's not some peripheral add-on—and it's also more likely to be sustained."

But in seeking the biggest bang for their buck by backing programs or bolstering ideas that already have currency, foundations often attend carefully to the work other funders support. Broad, for instance, is echoing Gates' lead into the area of teacher support (although Broad has its own to-do list). And it's no coincidence that the bloom of the small-schools movement in New York City prospered with infusions of Gates money, earlier in the Bloomberg administration, and has tapered as Gates redirected its funding streams to other areas, like teacher evaluation and developing schools for older, under-achieving students.

Edward Pauly, who directs research and evaluation at Wallace, said, "Nobody elected foundations to make policy or allocate public dollars." In a pure research environment, political concerns wouldn't shadow economic investments—but in the real world of education reform, they do.

Lippert acknowledges the bottom-line truth of Gates' assertion, that private money is relatively puny compared to public education funding, but says "it's the most worthwhile category of investment that exists, because the future health of our economy, our democracy, and our citizenry depend largely on whether our public schools succeed."

# 7

# Large Class Sizes Are Unfair to Students

*Scott Thill*

*Scott Thill runs the online magazine* Morphizm.com. *His writing has appeared in* Wired, Salon, XLR8R, Alternet, *and* LA Weekly.

*The proposal by billionaire Bill Gates to increase class size in America's schools in order to increase achievement levels flies in the face of research and common sense. It is also hypocritical given that Gates sends his own children to private schools that tout smaller class sizes as a selling point. Gates' current position is even further at odds with his own foundation's small school initiative in New York which promoted smaller high schools as a way of increasing graduation rates, and seems to have achieved this goal.*

Once dominant, now America is just average when it comes to education. Its public solution, recently communicated by Microsoft mogul Bill Gates? Increased class sizes, decreased teacher counts, fewer advanced degrees, and probably more mediocrity.

It's the type of technocratic cure-all one would expect Gates to champion, and it will doubtless perform as lamely as Microsoft, which currently hobbles at $30 a share while its more intuitive tech rivals like Apple and Google respectively hover around $200 to $600. But Gates' short-changing of the

Scott Thill, "Where Does Billionaire Monopolist Bill Gates Get Off Saying Bigger Class and Fewer Teachers Is the Education Solution?," *Alternet*, December 17, 2010. © 2010 by Independent Media Institute. All rights reserved. Used by permission.

nation's education system is just another strain of neoconservative austerity going viral in our global village. And it's just as short-sighted as the disaster capitalism that destroyed America's economic integrity: Increasing America's class sizes and downsizing its teachers could cost us more than it could save us.

"Bringing the United States up to the average performance of Finland, the best-performing education system, could result in gains in the order of 103 trillion dollars," claimed the Organization for Economic Cooperation and Development's [OECD] three-year Programme for International Student Assessment report released in December. Of course, those are just the numbers. The hypocrisy stings worse.

"The oligarchy making decisions for public-school kids—like Michael Bloomberg and Bill Gates—send their own children to private schools with comparatively tiny class sizes of 15 or less, while many of the kids in the schools they impose their policies on have classes of 25, 30 or more," Leonie Haimson, executive director for the nonprofit educational watchdog Class Size Matters, told *AlterNet*. "New York City children are now suffering from the largest class sizes in early grades since 1999, despite billions more spent on education. And class sizes are expected to increase again next year."

*[I]f you follow the money, it leads to very rich people who have two sets of educational standards: One for their kids, and another for ours.*

## Larger Class Sizes Are Unfair

Let them, Gates has argued. According to the *New York Times* and the Associated Press, both Gates and the Bill and Melinda Gates Foundation's CEO Jeff Raikes have floated the theory that teachers trump class size when it comes to educational excellence. The jackpot comes when you reward effective

teachers with higher pay, they argue, regardless of their senior-
ity or advanced degrees. Which means, in the real world outside of the fuzzy jargon, rewarding those who can pass their
students and satisfy technocrats hypnotized by what the
American Federation of Teachers [AFT] called "quickie observations or crude test-score calculations masquerading as
teacher evaluations."

"For those of us who represent teachers on the frontlines,
the issue is how this translates to the day-to-day realities of
teaching kids," explained an AFT statement targeted at Gates'
sales pitch, which has also been parroted by U.S. Secretary of
Education Arne Duncan in an ironically titled speech called
"Bang for the Buck in Schooling." "What kind of future are we
creating for our kids if education policies, however well-
intentioned, result in larger classes and in teachers with less
experience?"

One that is similar to the educational present, one would
argue, only worse. According to the OECD, the United States
is simply average in reading and science but below-average in
math, not a good show for a declining empire convinced of its
economic policies. With tax-cut compromises hammering
Americans already besieged by a worsening unemployment
nightmare, arguments over class size are trending toward class
warfare. The United States already boasts the largest average
class sizes outside of Asia, and those classes are inequitably
distributed among the poor and people of color. Not a good
show for the first African-American president in U.S. history,
whose administration is looking to increase schools' storage
capacity and hoping on a return on investment.

But if you follow the money, it leads to very rich people
who have two sets of educational standards: One for their
kids, and another for ours.

"They want to fire experienced teachers because they cost
more, increase class size, and commit our kids to online learn-

ing—none of which they would consider for their own children," said Haimson. "It is the height of hypocrisy."

The AFT quickly tore apart Gates and Duncan's core data. Their austerity measures were based on the fragile assumptions that teacher experience has little correlation to student achievement, postgraduate study is negligible, and that class size doesn't really matter. But experience is everything in any field, pay raises are primary when it comes to retaining hires, and the advanced study of one's field is what keeps you from being shamefully passed up by countries like snowy Finland when it comes to educational excellence.

AFT's own proposals were common-sense suggestions for lowered recession expectations: More funded preschooling to close the achievement gap between the rich and the poor, community-minded schools that also dispense career and degree counseling as well as medical care, and a shared responsibility for educational achievement with the parents, the state and its policies. AFT's research has shown that decreased class sizes result in more graduates, who generate net cost savings of $168,000 per student. Sounds like a smart-money suggestion for the body politic, rather than just the rich. So what's the problem?

"If class sizes in public schools increase, parents with resources may simply leave public schools, choosing charter schools and private schools in hopes of finding smaller classes for their children," the AFT said.

That argument seems to synchronize with the Bill and Melinda Gates Foundation's education mission, which is "to ensure that all students graduate from high school ready for college and career and prepared to complete a postsecondary degree or certificate with value in the workplace." But it's hard to square that last promise with Gates and Duncan's argument that advanced degrees don't matter in the educational long run.

Much harder to reconcile its position on class size, when the Gates Foundation's small-school initiative in New York, which services 100 high-school students per *grade*, has resulted in increased graduation rates. That data came after a decade of experience, and hundreds of millions donated by the Gates Foundation, Carnegie Corporation, Open Society Institute and more. The Gates Foundation recently launched a nine-city partnership between local school districts and public charter schools, which together will probably discover that charter and private school students often outperform public school students because charter and private school classes are often smaller.

It's a no-brainer, wrote Haimson in *The 7 Myths of Class Size Reduction.* "Studies from Tennessee, Wisconsin, and states throughout the country have demonstrated that students who are assigned to smaller classes in grades K-3rd do better in every way that can be measured," she explained. "They score higher on tests, receive better grades, and exhibit improved attendance."

---

*In order to truly compete in a global marketplace bypassing your fading empire, you have to share both the wins and losses, standing united for all.*

---

## More Economic Equality Would Result in a Stronger American Society

So this debate isn't really about the data, or its correlations, but rather the money. Rather than raise taxes—or even end tax-cuts for the rich, and inject some much-needed revenue into America's so-called economic recovery—technocratic liberals and conservatives have opted to drive an ever-larger wedge between the haves and have-nots. The haves get corporate-funded charter schools with smaller classes, more graduates, and better returns on investment. The have-nots get holding pens for the poor. There's no data in the universe that would argue this approach will best serve the public, just limited albeit powerful interest.

The true solutions to America's education nightmare, and its recession, are economically simple and have proven their experience. And they don't benefit just the rich, but us all. In order to truly compete in a global marketplace bypassing your fading empire, you have to share both the wins and the losses, standing united for all. Or else you'll end up losers.

"The solution is to reorganize the economy so the benefits of growth are more widely shared," explained economist Robert Reich. "Exempt the first $20,000 of income from payroll taxes, and apply payroll taxes to incomes over $250,000. Extend Medicare to all. Extend the Earned Income Tax Credit all the way up through families earning $50,000. Make higher education free to families that now can't afford it. Rehire teachers."

# 8

# US Colleges Lack the Rigor Needed to Compete Globally

*Richard Arum and Josipa Roksa*

*Richard Arum and Josipa Roksa co-authored the book* Academically Adrift: Limited Learning on College Campuses *published in 2011. Richard Arum is professor of sociology in New York University's Department of Sociology and professor of education in NYU's Steinhardt School of Culture, Education, and Human Development. Josipa Roksa is an assistant professor of sociology at the University of Virginia.*

*Colleges are not providing students with a rigorous education that challenges them to do more than just show up. Instead they have moved to a service model of education, allowing students to pick and choose classes according to their own desires as opposed to what will push students to excel and learn more than what they already know.*

*Many institutions have lost focus on their primary mission of educating undergraduate students. Colleges and students need to hold themselves more accountable for insuring a diploma has some value after graduation.*

As this year's [2011] crop of college graduates leaves school, burdened with high levels of debt and entering a severely depressed job market, they may be asking themselves a fundamental question: Was college worth it?

Richard Arum and Josipa Roksa, "College, Too Easy for Its Own Good," *Los Angeles Times*, June 2, 2011. © 2011 by Richard Arum. All rights reserved. Used by permission of the author.

And it's no wonder they're asking. Large numbers of the new graduates will face sustained periods of underemployment and low wages for years. Worse still, many of them were poorly prepared for the future, having spent four (or more) years of college with only modest academic demands that produced only limited improvement in the skills necessary to be successful in today's knowledge-based economy.

We recently tracked several thousand students as they moved through and graduated from a diverse set of more than two dozen colleges and universities, and we found consistent evidence that many students were not being appropriately challenged. In a typical semester, 50% of students did not take a single course requiring more than 20 pages of writing, 32% did not have any classes that required reading more than 40 pages per week, and 36% reported studying alone five or fewer hours per week.

---

*At many schools, students can choose from a menu of easy programs and classes that allow them to graduate without having received a rigorous college education.*

---

Not surprisingly, given such a widespread lack of academic rigor, about a third of students failed to demonstrate significant gains in critical thinking, complex reasoning and writing ability (as measured by the Collegiate Learning Assessment) during their four years of college.

The students themselves must bear some of the blame for this, of course. Improvement in thinking and writing skills requires academic engagement; simply hanging out on a college campus for multiple years isn't enough. Yet at many institutions, that seems to be sufficient to earn a degree. At many schools, students can choose from a menu of easy programs and classes that allow them to graduate without having received a rigorous college education. Colleges are complicit, in that they reward students with high grades for little effort. Indeed, the students in our study who reported studying alone five or fewer hours per week nevertheless had an average cumulative GPA of 3.16.

To be sure, there were many exceptions to this dismal portrait of the state of undergraduate learning. Some academic programs and colleges are quite rigorous, and some students we followed pushed themselves and excelled. In general, traditional arts and science fields (math, science, humanities and the social sciences) tended to be more demanding, and students who majored in those subjects studied more and showed higher gains. So too did students attending more selective colleges. In addition, at every college and university examined, we found some students who were applying themselves and learning at impressive levels.

---

*Many institutions favor priorities that can be boasted about in alumni magazines and admission brochures or that can help boost their scores in college rankings.*

---

## Higher Education Is Failing Students

These real accomplishments do not, however, exonerate the colleges and universities that are happy to collect annual tuition dollars but then fail to provide many students with a high-quality education.

In much of higher education, the problem is in part that undergraduate education is no longer a top priority. Instead of focusing on undergraduates and what they are learning, schools have come to care more about such things as admission yields, graduation rates, faculty research productivity, pharmaceutical patents, deluxe dormitory rooms, elaborate student centers and state-of-the-art athletic facilities complete with luxury boxes. Many institutions favor priorities that can be boasted about in alumni magazines and admission brochures or that can help boost their scores in college rankings.

Colleges have abandoned responsibility for shaping students' academic development and instead have come to embrace a service model that caters to satisfying students' expressed desires.

These trends have all added up to less rigor. California labor economists Philip Babcock and Mindy Marks, for example, have documented that full-time college students' time spent studying dropped in half between 1960 and today. Moreover, from 1970 to 2000, as colleges increasingly hired additional staff to attend to student social and personal needs, the percentage of professional employees in higher education who were faculty decreased from about two-thirds to around one-half. At the same time, through their professional advancement and tenure policies, schools encouraged faculty to focus more on research rather than teaching. When teaching was considered as part of the equation, student course assessments tended to be the method used to evaluate teaching, which tends to incentivize lenient grading and entertaining forms of instruction.

So how should this academic drift of our colleges and universities be addressed? Some have proposed introducing a federal accountability system. We are against such a move, as federal regulation would probably be counterproductive and include a large set of detrimental, unintended consequences.

## Accountability Is Needed to Ensure Success

Accountability in higher education rightly resides at lower levels of the system. College trustees have at the institutional level the fiduciary responsibility to begin holding administrators accountable by asking: How are student learning outcomes and program quality being measured, and what is being done to address areas of concern that have been identified? Faculty must also take responsibility individually and collectively to define and ensure program quality and academic standards. Finally, student undergraduate cultures will have to change, with students themselves recognizing that they need more from college than a paper diploma and an expanded roster of Facebook friends.

# 9

# US Students Trail Global Peers in Foreign Language Learning

*Lewis Beale*

*Lewis Beale is a writer whose work has appeared in* The New York Times, Los Angeles Times, Washington Post, *and* Newsday.

*Public schools in America have never seriously focused on the study of foreign languages as an essential part of student education. Evidence of this is found in how often foreign language instruction is one of the first programs cut when school budgets shrink. Other countries, often by mandate, require their children to learn English to supplement their native language. And some require a third language, affording their students a flexibility in the global job market that American students lack. Although some organizations, including the US Departments of Education and Defense, are beginning to recognize the failure of America's foreign language programs, too often language study remains a choice for a few rather than a mandate for the many.*

All you need to know about the study of foreign languages in the United States is that many more middle and high school students are studying the dead language spoken by Caesar and Nero than such critically important tongues as Chinese, Arabic, Hindi, Farsi, Japanese, Russian and Urdu combined.

"Things cannot get worse. We are at the bottom of the barrel now" in terms of foreign language study in America's schools, says Nancy Rhodes of the Center for Applied Linguistics, which surveys language study in the nation's schools every 10 years.

The center's most recent report shows a decrease in the last decade in school language programs, which Rhodes says can be attributed to "budget cuts, and foreign languages are among the first things that get cut. They are seen as something that's not a necessity. And another reason is the No Child Left Behind legislation—about a third of our schools report they have been negatively affected because of the focus on math and reading scores."

Unlike Europe, where more than 90 percent of children begin learning English in elementary school, and several countries mandate the teaching of two foreign languages in upper secondary school, America has never placed a premium on teaching foreign languages. Less than one-third of American elementary schools offer foreign language courses, and less than half of all middle and high school students are enrolled in such classes, the majority studying Spanish.

---

*There is ... a feeling, much too common in the United States, that language education is not for everyone ....*

---

## Foreign Languge Instruction Is Only Recently Compelling

Key reasons for this disparity include geography and Americans' sense of cultural chauvinism.

"We have never had a compelling reason to interact with the rest of the world," says Marty Abbott of the American Council on the Teaching of Foreign Languages. "We have been isolated geographically, and haven't had that urgency [to learn other languages] that Europeans have had."

"[Other] countries recognize that language is a tool for economic competitiveness and national security, so they have mandatory language programs," says Shuhan Wang of the National Foreign Language Center. "We have xenophobia and are always trying to use English as a badge of national identity and expression," but because English is perceived as a global language, "it becomes a two-edged sword. People understand us, but we don't comprehend them. We are losing so much and are not aware of it."

There is also a feeling, much too common in the United States, that language education is not for everyone, and as Abbott says, it's "just not normal." And for a long time in the U.S., the teaching of languages was more of an academic exercise, a rote recitation of grammatical rules, separate from the goal of actually going out and speaking to someone.

Yet the picture is not totally bleak. Even though, for example, Chinese and Arabic are still taught in only a fraction of America's schools—approximately 4 percent and 1 percent, respectively—their growth has been statistically significant over the past 10 years.

"There are many more Arabic programs in K-12," says Karin Ryding of the American Association of Teachers of Arabic, "but there is not any official survey of how many schools are teaching Arabic and to what extent." Surveys also fail catch how many students may study languages through their religious or cultural institutions.

Ryding adds that a number of factors have held back Arabic education in the past. The alphabet is different, and teachers have generally emerged from the Arab-American community, many of them not particularly experienced. There is also no certification system for teachers of Arabic, and curriculum materials are lacking. Plus, Ryding says, "there is also an issue with Arab culture: Most Americans don't understand it; they consider it exotic."

Some of the same issues affect Chinese (Mandarin) language study. "It is a non-Roman alphabet, and that adds linguistic distance," says Wang. "It's also a cultural distance."

Yet because of China's increasing economic clout, more and more schools are teaching the language. Part of this has been spurred by Hanban, a Chinese government-sponsored language and cultural initiative, which has been providing qualified teachers to American schools, as well as promoting in-China language programs for teachers and students. There is also some funding from the U.S. Department of Education for so-called "critical language" study, which includes Mandarin.

"We're seeing Chinese in the same situation we saw Japanese in the '80s," Abbott says. "The Japanese economy was really strong then, and when we see a threat from another economy, the push [to learn that language] is strong."

There is, of course, still plenty of catching up to do—according to a 2006 Department of Education study, 200 million Chinese schoolchildren were studying English, while only 24,000 of their American peers were learning Chinese. That number has increased over the past few years, but the gap is still huge.

---

*Parents are starting to push for more language study, particularly in the elementary schools, and not always in areas expected.*

---

That federal study was co-sponsored by U.S. Department of Defense and the director of National Intelligence, perhaps not surprising given the military and intelligence communities' problems in the war on terror. In announcing the report's accompanying National Security Language Initiative, President George W. Bush pictured the American language deficit as a security issue. "This initiative is a broad-gauged initiative that deals with the defense of the country, the diplomacy of the country, the intelligence to defend our country and the education of our people," he told a collection of university presidents in 2006.

Despite the rhetoric and language about starting at kindergarten, the program currently focuses on scholarships to send American high school students overseas to study Arabic, Mandarin, Hindi, Korean, Persian (Farsi), Russian and Turkish. Their numbers are measured in the hundreds.

## Recent Trends Show Promise

And yet, experts in the field believe that overall, things are looking up. Children in our increasingly multicultural society are finding that one way to learn about other cultures is through their languages. Parents are starting to push for more language study, particularly in the elementary schools, and not always in areas expected. Private language academies are popping up all over the country, and online learning is taking off. There is also a slow but growing feeling among firms that manufacture or sell overseas that language skills are an important business tool.

All of which means that language education is, in fact, "a force, not a choice," says Wang. "Sooner or later we will have to deal with it, and confront the issue that we are so far behind in language studies."

# 10

# College Access Is Shrinking Despite Demand for an Educated Workforce

*Kim Clark*

*Kim Clark is a journalist with more than 20 years of experience. She specializes in writing about college financial aid, personal finance, business, and economics, and has written for U.S. News and World Report since 1998. She was a Kiplinger Fellow at The Ohio State University in 2007.*

*American colleges and universities are struggling to serve their students in the midst of major funding cuts brought on by a lingering recession and decreased tax revenue. As a persistently high unemployment rate finds many unemployed Americans eager to further their education in order to find work, schools in many states are unable to provide the classes and programs students need in order to graduate.*

*While some schools are rising to the challenge and using creativity to cut costs without affecting student offerings, other schools are simply increasing class sizes and reducing the number of classes available. The net result for those schools is an inferior education that takes longer to complete, leaving many to wonder if college degrees will really be of any benefit in a shrinking jobs market.*

Kim Clark, "Budget Cuts Take Toll on Education," *U.S. News & World Report*, August 19, 2009. ©2009 by U.S. News & World Report. All rights reserved. Reproduced by permission.

Every chair was taken. Yet more students jammed into the classroom for the first summer session class of City College of San Francisco's [CCSF] Microcomputer Applications for Business 101. By the time the class started, at least 12 extra people were standing in the aisles and clustered in the doorway. Instructor Hugo Aparicio shouted to the growing crowd that there were only enough computers to accommodate 28 students. Normally, with so many eager learners, CCSF would hire an instructor to teach another section of the class. But the state's $26 billion-plus deficit means there's no money for extra teachers. So Aparicio announced that only the first 28 students who registered for the course could stay. One young woman began to weep, explaining that this course was the last one she needed to graduate. Sophomore Inga Jargal also pleaded. She was having trouble finding *any* class to fill up her schedule: If she couldn't enroll in another one, she might lose her financial aid and campus job in the registrar's office. It was no use. There simply wasn't room. So, in a scene that is being repeated increasingly in California and other recession-socked states, several otherwise qualified students were sent out into the dark, blustery evening.

"I am worried," says Jargal. "I need an education for my future and my son's future," says the 26-year-old single mom.

*Colleges are not using the recession as a spur for the kinds of fundamental changes needed to give more Americans better training.*

## College Access Is Endangered

The recession, state budget cuts, and hidebound bureaucracies are endangering some of the most important foundations of the American dream—the low-cost, high-quality public colleges created to provide anyone with smarts and diligence the training needed to succeed.

True, a few public higher ed leaders are using the financial downturn as a catalyst to permanently lower costs and increase the graduation rate above today's unimpressive 55 percent. They are reducing waste, streamlining, and modernizing courses.

But some influential analysts say too many colleges are reacting in shortsighted ways that will undermine the institutions themselves, as well as the opportunities for socioeconomic mobility that are at the core of American society. Just when public colleges are being swamped by applicants eager for low-cost classes and the nation needs new ideas to pull the economy out of recession, many schools are shutting classroom doors, raising tuition, crowding courses, canceling extracurriculars, and hobbling research.

"This is an opportunity," says William Bowen, a former Princeton University president who has written several books examining inequities and quality problems in higher education. "Some sensible pruning is occurring. Some good could come out of this." But, he worries, colleges are not using the recession as a spur for the kinds of fundamental changes needed to give more Americans better training.

The financial troubles of community colleges and state universities are far more important than the layoffs at elite schools such as Harvard and Yale that have grabbed headlines. Such storied privates educate perhaps 2 percent of America's 18.3 million college students. Public colleges teach 74 percent.

## Budget Cuts May Be the Last Straw for Many Schools

The immediate crisis was sparked by an estimated 5 percent—about $4 billion—drop in the amount of money state governments apportioned to higher education for the fiscal year that started July 1 [2009]. Federal stimulus money can close only part of that gap this year [2009].

A drop of a few billion dollars out of the $79 billion or so that states had spent on higher education in 2008 might not sound severe, but for many colleges, this was a last straw. Even during the boom years, most states weren't increasing college budgets to match rising enrollments. The average public research university got almost $8,350 per student from taxpayers in 2002. By 2006, that had dropped below $7,100, according to the Delta Project on Postsecondary Education Costs, Productivity, and Accountability.

Now, public colleges are receiving even less per student. In hard-hit states such as California, Nevada, and Oregon, where colleges have had to slash their budgets by double-digit percentages in the past few months, educational and political leaders say they don't have the time or money to do anything but turn away more students. In California, where tax revenues for higher education are expected to plunge by about $2 billion, the flagship University of California system reduced its incoming freshman class this year [2009] by 2,300 and will probably have to reduce it by thousands more in 2010. The schools that are supposed to take the UC overflow, the California State University system, cut enrollment by about 4,000 students this year [2009] and are likely to cut 10 times as many next year. The CSU overflow students, along with thousands of unemployed workers hoping for retraining, have been mobbing community colleges. California community college leaders say they simply can't accommodate the influx with a state budget reduction of more than $340 million. They fear they could end up turning away as many as 250,000 students in the coming months.

That's effectively trapping thousands of Californians, like 20-year-old Sarah Hendrickson, into unemployment or low-paying, dead-end jobs. Hendrickson, who is wrapping up her associate's degree at a community college in San Luis Obispo, says she broke down in tears when her adviser told her she couldn't transfer into the overcrowded local state university for at least another year. "I am kind of stuck in all aspects of my life," she says.

California is the most extreme case, but many other states are closing classroom doors by raising tuition or cutting aid. In Florida, where the higher education budget this year [2009] is $153 million, or 4 percent, lower than last year's, many public universities will hike tuition by 15 percent. A year at Stony Brook University in New York, where state legislators have required public colleges to send some of their tuition money to the state's general fund to reduce the deficit, will cost students at least $1,000 more this year [2009]. The state of Washington, which has reduced its higher education budget by $168 million, or 10.6 percent, will raise tuition at public universities by about 14 percent this year. Washington's governor, Christine Gregoire, says that raising tuition was the least bad of all the options to make up a $9 billion shortfall over the next two years.

---

*The recession is making classes harder to get into, more expensive—and, possibly, less instructive.*

---

Although the federal government has increased the number and size of the need-based Pell grants and made it easier to take out and repay federally backed loans, many states, such as Florida and West Virginia, are reining in their financial aid programs. The net result is that the true cost of college for many students is rising at a time when they have less money.

Jon Shure, a tax expert at the Washington-based Center on Budget and Policy Priorities, says state officials and taxpayers used to "subsidize students because that was in the best interests of society. Now the balance is shifting to where students pay more and taxpayers less." That will mean some low-income students who could benefit from college will either be priced out or will hobble themselves with education debt, he says.

The recession is making classrooms harder to get into, more expensive—and, possibly, less instructive. Many colleges are saving money by packing more students into fewer courses. Arizona public universities, for example, have laid off thousands of employees and canceled scores of classes and programs in the past year. "You definitely learn less," University of Arizona junior Kevin Ferguson says of his bigger classes. "You can't interact with the professor when you are contending with 200 to 300 other students." Instructors say increased class sizes mean they work many more unpaid hours and have much less time to do, for example, thoughtful grading of papers, let alone research. Instructors' time shortages are being worsened by many colleges' requirements that staffers take unpaid furlough days.

Even seemingly small cuts might threaten the quality of education. The Kentucky community college system has decided not to offer tenure to new hires, prompting outcries that the system will lose the best candidates, who prefer colleges that offer more job security. Florida State University pulled the phones out of English and history professors' offices, saving more than $12,000 a year but sparking complaints that it will be harder for students to reach professors.

## Courses and Programs Are Being Cancelled

The cuts also mean fewer choices and opportunities for students. Many colleges are deciding that they can no longer fund less popular courses. Idaho State University, like many other schools, has eliminated some low-enrollment courses such as French, German, Russian, Arabic, and Chinese. Many other schools have eliminated expensive science classes. The University of Nevada-Las Vegas—fictional hometown of television's *CSI*—has decided to phase out its forensic science program. Others are targeting the arts: Washington State University is disbanding its theater program. The University of

West Georgia has canceled some music courses. "I don't believe I've ever seen a more troubling situation" for college music students across the country, says Mark Camphouse, interim chair of George Mason University's music department.

Activities, too, are disappearing. Florida International University [FIU] and Minnesota State University-Mankato eliminated bands. FIU also zeroed out the budget for its cheerleading squad. Many schools are canceling expensive and untelevised sports teams such as baseball, skiing, wrestling, and swimming. At least 10 schools, including Indiana State and Missouri Southern, have canceled their tennis teams so far this year.

Such classroom and activity cuts are drawing increasing criticism from students and faculty who point to what they consider to be continued wasteful extravagance. Florida Atlantic University [FAU] laid off five computer science and engineering professors, but it is proceeding with construction on a new movie theater. (FAU officials say the construction is funded with donated and earmarked funds that couldn't be used for operations.)

North Carolina's legislature has ordered public universities to cut their budgets by about 10 percent but is still having taxpayers pick up almost $14 million worth of tuition for out-of-state students, including athletes. Amy Perko, executive director of the Knight Commission on Intercollegiate Athletics, says many other recession-strapped colleges are spending millions on coaches and stadiums in the hopes of recouping big bucks from television contracts or alumni donations. But NCAA research shows that's a loser's bet, Perko says. "In 2006, only 19 of the 119 programs in the most competitive division finished the year with positive net revenue," she noted. The average shortfalls of nearly $9 million were subsidized by students and taxpayers, she says.

## Creative Solutions Have Helped Avoid Drastic Cuts

The news isn't all dire. A few oil-rich states—such as Texas, Alaska, and North Dakota—are increasing their spending on higher education. And several hard-hit states, such as Michigan and Ohio, have managed so far to avoid drastic cuts at universities.

*A few educational visionaries are experimenting with radical course redesigns to save money and give more students a better shot at graduating.*

Many colleges are turning the cutbacks into an opportunity to shed luxuries that had become common during fat years. Just by reducing the number of support staff who travel with sports teams, ending the indiscriminate handing out of "participation awards" to student athletes, and canceling some social activities, the universities belonging to the Pac-10 sports conference figure they'll collectively save about $1 million. The University of Texas athletic department estimates it will save at least $300,000 by replacing its glossy media guide booklets with DVDs. Athletes around the country are now taking buses to many games, instead of chartered planes. During the winter, the State University of New York-Canton saved approximately $250,000 by turning thermostats down to 68 Monday through Thursday and a frosty 58 on Fridays, when there were no classes. East Carolina University saved $30,000 by switching from paper to electronic tuition bills. The University of Vermont cut its custodial budget by $400,000 in part by making professors empty their own trash bins.

Many university executives are attempting to reduce the impact on students and lead by example by absorbing some of the financial pain themselves. The leadership of the University of Tennessee voluntarily took a 5 percent pay cut and turned in the keys to university cars to save the campus $400,000.

Arizona State University President Michael Crow donated his $60,000 bonus for 2008 to the university's financial aid office and took the same 15 unpaid furlough days as the rest of the executive staff in the first half of 2009.

A few educational visionaries are experimenting with radical course redesigns to save money and give more students a better shot at graduating. Robert Olin, dean of arts and sciences at the University of Alabama, has overseen the creation of a math lab that has revolutionized entry-level classes. No longer do students spend three or four hours a week listening to lectures, only to then do homework on their own. In the new classes, students get only 40 minutes of lecture a week but then do at least three hours of practice on specially programmed computers in the math lab, where there are lots of tutors to answer questions.

The new math courses cost the university about $82 per student—about two thirds of the cost of a traditional lecture class. But the pupils score higher on standardized end-of-course tests because they've had so much practice and individual attention, Olin says.

About 150 other schools, including the University of Massachusetts-Amherst, Arizona State, and the State University of New York system, are experimenting with similar redesigns of courses for everything from chemistry to Spanish, often with similar results. Cheaper, better classes are the only long-term solution to the growing demand for education and shrinking funding, says Carol Twigg, founder of the National Center for Academic Transformation.

The economy will some day rebound, of course. But those colleges that are just cutting courses or having instructors lecture in front of ever bigger classes will simply offer lower quality. They won't have solved the structural problems that have led to high costs and low graduation rates. "Thinking differently," Twigg says, "is the only solution."

# 11

# Education Budget Cuts Forecast a Less Prepared Workforce

*Gary Scharrer*

*Gary Scharrer is a writer for the* San Antonio Express-News.

*Budget cuts to education funding can have disastrous effects that will reverberate for years. Students in programs that are considered "extras" such as gifted and talented, early childhood education, and teen parenting education are being left behind, and cuts to grant funding for college students will make it more difficult to obtain a college degree.*

*The State of Texas faces such a scenario. Massive proposed spending cuts will assuredly result in severe future challenges for the state. An under-educated population places extra burdens on social services when people do not have the skills needed to compete in the workforce and earn the type of salary necessary to support themselves and their families.*

For Texans to understand the state's grim future, it might require all 1,030 school superintendents to immediately cancel high school sports—including Friday night football.

Of course, doing so might get them all fired, demographer Steve Murdock said.

So while the lights will continue shining on Texas high school football fields this fall [2011], he said, problems triggered by the state's budget crisis won't—a message he intends to take today to lawmakers.

By 2040, he will tell them, three in 10 Texas workers won't have even high school diplomas unless state leaders address the current trend line. Education is the only remedy for the coming crisis, he said, and the early budget plans would make the trend line much worse.

In short, public education stands to lose about $11.5 billion from current funding levels, cuts that would lead to larger class sizes and the loss of tens of thousands of jobs for teachers and education support staff.

The proposed budget also would whack "gifted and talented" programs, early childhood intervention, teen parenting education, reading, math and science initiatives and programs intended to help students stay in school, such as Communities in Schools. And the budget doesn't include money for new textbooks.

## Public Education Is in Crisis

"I am very concerned," said Murdock, a Rice University sociology professor and the former state demographer who served as U.S. Census Bureau director in the [President] George W. Bush administration. "It's not like we have a lot of slack in the system where we can slip a little bit and still be OK."

Murdock is particularly concerned about the two programs he says are most critical for addressing the woeful trend line: High quality pre-kindergarten and TEXAS grants, which he considers the building blocks for elevating education.

Yet both pre-K and TEXAS grant programs face severe budget cuts and could make the state's future challenges even more severe, he said.

The preliminary House budget plan would cut about $222 million out of pre-K funding over the next two years—affecting about 101,000 children currently in the full-day program. The TEXAS grant program faces a 41 percent budget cut, dropping the number of students who get college financial help from nearly 87,000 to 27,000.

Economists and business leaders also have looked at pre-K research and understand that high quality pre-K programs "address many of the problems we have in terms of education, a better work force, more skilled people, better high school and college completion rates," said Libby Doggett, deputy director for The Pew Center on the States.

House Public Education Chairman Rob Eissler, R-The Woodlands, said he can't defend the proposed cuts in pre-K and TEXAS grant funding and emphasized that it remains early in the process.

---

*Education is the single best predictor of income . . . and the combination of explosive Hispanic population growth and low academic achievement produces a sour forecast.*

---

"I'm just dealing with them and making the best of what we can. The whole theme is to fund the future," Eissler said.

The final budget could be months away.

"We have some serious, serious decisions to make," Eissler said. "We're starting in a tight place. If you predict the future based on today, it's not bright."

Minority children now make up at least 66 percent of the state's 4.8 million public school enrollment—and most children come from low-income families. Over the past 10 years, the number of children from low-income families has increased by 893,055, surpassing the overall enrollment growth during the same period.

## Funding for Education Is Needed for Long-Term Success

Education is the single best predictor of income, Murdock said, and the combination of explosive Hispanic population growth and low academic achievement produces a sour forecast.

The typical Texan today must be viewed from two per-spectives, he said: The average Anglo is a 40- to 44-year-old woman (beyond child-rearing years) with at least a junior college education, living in a household with income of $60,000 (2009)—with no appreciable change since 1999.

The other typical Texan, Murdock said, is a Hispanic male between 25 to 29 years old with a high school diploma or, often times, less than a high school diploma. That Texan lives in a household with income of $35,000 (2009)—down from $38,000 in 1999, Murdock said.

---

*Cutting education spending is like mortgaging the state's future. . . .*

---

Cutting pre-K programs and TEXAS grants, which help students finance college costs, could push Texas back even further, he said.

"We are lagging now and to fail to educate this population is a formula for long-term disaster for Texas," Murdock said.

The consensus of pre-K research is that pre-K investment is the best place to spend education money because it delivers the greatest return, said Ed Fuller, an education researcher at the University of Texas at Austin.

Cutting education spending is like mortgaging the state's future, he said, and will take years to recover.

"It's so backwards thinking," Fuller said. "Essentially, we're going to end up with two groups of people—one who can afford to have their kids educated and a much larger group of Texans who can't afford to have their kids educated."

In the long run, Texas will lose money as struggling students drop out, he said. They end up paying fewer taxes and requiring more social services or end up incarcerated, he said.

# 12

# The United States Must Produce Better Teachers to Compete Globally

## Judith Kleinfeld

*Judith Kleinfeld is the director of the Northern Studies program and a professor of psychology at the University of Alaska Fairbanks.*

*The quality of American teachers does not stack up when compared to countries that outperform the United States on international achievement tests. Increased rigor in the teacher education selection process is key. This coupled with more social prestige and competitive compensation can result in a higher quality of students choosing to pursue a career in teaching. Other countries hold their teachers in high esteem and allow only the brightest to enter the teaching profession. Higher academic achievement proves this is a strategy that works. Quality teachers produce quality students.*

A friend of mine is looking for a good school for his daughter. He has seen a lot of excellent teaching, particularly in private schools.

He observed one private school teacher who did not have the usual teaching credentials but he did have a Ph.D. in mathematics. He made mathematical concepts crystal clear, and his students were performing far above their grade level.

Judith Kleinfeld, "US Needs to Produce Better Teachers," *Anchorage Daily News*, September 15, 2011. © 2011 by Judith Kleinfeld. Reproduced by permission of the author. All rights reserved.

My friend's search for the finest education for his daughter led to his discovery of a study called "Closing the talent gap: Attracting and retaining top-third graduates to careers in education" (September, 2010) by the highly respected McKinsey and Company, which does international research for government and big corporations.

This report analyzes education in three countries which produce students who score at the top in international tests—Finland, Singapore, and South Korea.

## Quality Teachers Make the Difference

The high quality of teachers made the difference, everywhere. Decades of educational research has come to the same conclusion.

In real estate, the saying goes, there are three rules: "Location, location, location!" You can say the same about schools. What is important is "Teachers, teachers, teachers!"

How do we find or create high quality teachers?

---

*"Don't even step on the shadow of a teacher," goes a Korean proverb.*

---

The McKinsey Report analyzes the way teacher preparation systems work in these three high achieving countries and tries to identify common factors:

*1) Selective admission to teacher training:* Take Finland, the country which comes out the highest in international tests of science, reading and mathematics. "Teachers are required to obtain a master's degree in a five-year program, and applicants are generally drawn from the top 20 percent of high school graduates." A rigorous selection process follows, based on many other factors.

"As a result, only about one in ten applicants is selected to be a teacher. Partly owing to its prestige, teaching is the most popular career choice and the most admired profession among students, outpolling law and medicine."

*2) Cultural respect accorded to teaching*: In each of these countries, teaching has enormous social prestige, due to pay, selectivity, and tradition. "Don't even step on the shadow of a teacher," goes a Korean proverb.

*3) Competitive compensation*: South Korea is the most extreme example. "Korean teachers' earnings place them between engineers and doctors with purchasing power in the local economy nearly 250 percent higher than that of American teachers."

*4) Professional working environment*: In Singapore, "a few senior and master teachers in each school observe and coach other teachers, prepare model lessons and materials, advise on teaching methods and best practices, organize training and support newly qualified teachers and trainees."

To create such conditions, each country has a high degree of government regulation on the national level. The United States, in contrast, has a complex, decentralized school system with educational control fragmented between national, state, and local organizations.

---

*With unemployment now close to 10 percent and the retirement of the baby boom generation, teaching is an attractive profession for many very accomplished people.*

---

Rather than take this complexity as an undesirable problem, we need to take a different route, taking advantage of our decentralized system's potential for experimentation. One example is Teach for America which recruits top college graduates, often from the best prestigious colleges. In a recent year, 46,000 students applied and fewer than 10 percent were accepted. The model can not be widely applied—these graduates teach only for two or three years—but the program does demonstrate that approaches can be found to recruit highly selected students.

Alternative routes to teaching are also proliferating. These are quite varied, work only in certain circumstances, and effectiveness is mixed. Nonetheless some approaches show a lot of promise.

With unemployment now close to 10 percent and the retirement of the baby boom generation, teaching is an attractive profession for many very accomplished people. My father was one. The high point of his career was teaching after he retired as an engineer. He could make complex subjects clear and use his practical experience to show how students would benefit from what they were learning. Late in life, he found his calling.

There is no silver bullet to creating great teachers, no panacea. But the McKinsey Report is right about what we should do—launch many experiments, accepting that many will fail but a few may succeed. For experimentation, our decentralized system gives America a great advantage.

# Organizations to Contact

*The editors have compiled the following list of organizations concerned with the issues debated in this book. The descriptions are derived from materials provided by the organizations. All have publications or information available for interested readers. The list was compiled on the date of publication of the present volume; names, addresses, phone and fax numbers, and e-mail and Internet addresses may change. Be aware that many organizations take several weeks or longer to respond to inquiries, so allow as much time as possible.*

**Alliance for Excellent Education**
1201 Connecticut Avenue NW, Suite 901
Washington, DC   20036
202-828-0828 • fax: 202-828-0821
website: www.all4ed.org

The Alliance for Excellent Education promotes high school transformation to make it possible for every child to graduate prepared for postsecondary learning and success in life. The Alliance focuses on America's six million most at-risk secondary school students—those in the lowest achievement quartile—who are most likely to leave school without a diploma or to graduate unprepared for a productive future. It publishes the biweekly newsletter, *Straight A's: Public Education Policy and Progress*, along with numerous reports on issues and policy.

**Center on Reinventing Public Education (CRPE)**
University of Washington Bothell, Seattle, WA   98195
206-685-2214 • fax: 206-221-7402
email crpe@u.washington.edu
website: www.crpe.org

CRPE engages in independent research and policy analysis on a range of K–12 public education reform issues, including school choice, productivity, teachers, urban district reform, leadership, and state and federal reform. CRPE's work is based on two premises: that public schools should be measured against the goal of educating all children well, and that current institutions too often fail to achieve this goal. Its research, including *Limited Capacity at the State Level: A Threat to Future School Improvement*, published in June 2011, seeks to understand complicated problems and to design innovative and practical solutions.

## Challenge Success

485 Lasuen Mall, Stanford, CA   94305-3096
email: info@challengesuccess.org
website: www.challengesuccess.org

Challenge Success, a project of the Stanford University School of Education, is a research-based intervention program focused on three core areas: school reform, parent education, and youth development. It works with parents, schools, and youth to encourage development of the skills for success that are often overlooked in the current education system—critical thinking, character, creativity, resilience, self-management, and engagement with learning. Challenge Success features a compilation of research on its website examining how narrow definitions of success adversely affect children.

## Education Sector

1201 Connecticut Avenue NW, Suite 850
Washington, DC   20036
202-552-2840 • fax: 202-775-5877
website: www.educationsector.org

Education Sector is an independent think tank that challenges conventional thinking in education policy. It is a nonprofit, nonpartisan organization committed to achieving a measurable impact in education policy, both by improving existing reform initiatives and by developing new, innovative solutions to the nation's most pressing education problems. Its website includes a section titled *Charts You Can Trust* that provides

graphical presentations of Sector research such as "Debt to Degree: A New Way of Measuring College Success," published in August 2011.

## The Education Trust

1250 H Street, N.W., Suite 700, Washington, DC   20005
202-293-1217 • fax: 202-293-2605
website: www.edtrust.org

The Education Trust promotes high academic achievement for all students at all levels. The goal of EdTrust is to work alongside educators, parents, students, policymakers, and civic and business leaders in communities across the country, providing practical assistance in their efforts to transform schools and colleges into institutions that serve all students well. Its April 2011 white paper, "Stuck Schools Revisited: Beneath the Averages," explores why current efforts are not enough to raise achievement and close performance gaps.

## Institute for Democratic Education in America (IDEA)

P.O. Box 452, Tarrytown, NY   10591
800-878-5740
email: info@democraticeducation.orq
website: http://democraticeducation.org

IDEA is a national nonprofit organization whose mission is to ensure that all young people can engage meaningfully with their education and gain the tools to build a just, democratic, and sustainable world. Founded by educators from across the country, IDEA is committed to bridging the gap between democratic values and the way society educates and treats young people. Its website features *The Eduvation Library*, a collaborative project to curate high-quality resources that support meaningful learning.

## National Education Association (NEA)

1201 16th St., NW, Washington, DC   20036-3290
(202) 833-4000 • fax: (202) 822-7974
website: www.nea.org

NEA is a professional employee organization open to any employee of public schools, colleges, and universities. At both the state and national level, NEA affiliates lobby legislators on behalf of its members and public schools in an effort to protect academic freedom, ensure the rights of school employees, and increase the effectiveness of public education. Among other stances, NEA supports the use of professional pay to recruit and retain quality teachers and works to ensure that the achievement gap of low-income and minority students is reduced. *NEA Today* is the monthly magazine of the NEA.

## The Partnership for 21$^{st}$ Century Skills (P21)
1 Massachusetts Avenue, Suite 700, Washington, DC   20001
202-312-6429
email: tvarshavsky@p21.org
website: www.p21.org

P21 is a national organization that advocates for 21st-century readiness for every student. As the United States continues to compete in a global economy that demands innovation, the organization and its members provide tools and resources to help the US education system focus on critical thinking and problem solving, communication, collaboration, and creativity and innovation. The P21 website provides a document detailing its vision for student success in the new global economy titled: "Framework for 21$^{st}$ Century Learning".

## Rethinking Schools
1001 E. Keefe Avenue, Milwaukee, WI   53212
414-964-9646 • fax: 414-964-7220
email: office@rethinkingschools.org
website: www.rethinkingschools.org

Rethinking Schools began as a local effort to address issues such as standardized testing and a textbook-dominated curriculum. It is firmly committed to the vision that public education is central to the creation of a humane, caring, multiracial democracy. It publishes the quarterly magazine, *Rethinking Schools*, available on its website.

**United States Department of Education (ED)**
400 Maryland Ave., SW, Washington, DC   20202
(800) 872-5327
website: www.ed.gov

The US Department of Education was established by Congress
on May 4, 1980, with the goal of improving education nationwide through the use of federally mandated education programs. Initiatives by ED have focused on increasing the accountability of public schools and teachers, as well as
providing research and evaluation on school issues. ED publishes a variety of newsletters on specific topics relating to
education; all of these and other publications and reports by
the department can be accessed online.

# Bibliography

Richard Arum
and Josipa Roksa
*Academically Adrift: Limited Learning on College Campuses.* Chicago: The University of Chicago Press, 2011.

James Bellanca
and Ron Brandt
*21$^{st}$ Century Skills: Rethinking How Students Learn.* Bloomington, IN: Solution Tree, 2010.

Steven Brill
*Class Warfare: Inside the Fight to Fix America's Schools.* New York: Simon and Schuster, 2011.

Karin Chenoweth
*How It's Being Done: Urgent Lessons From Unexpected Schools.* Cambridge, MA: Harvard Education Press, 2009.

Amy Chua
*Battle Hymn of the Tiger Mother.* New York: Penguin Press, 2011.

David T. Conley
*College Knowledge: What it Really Takes for Students to Succeed and What We Can Do to Get Them Ready.* San Francisco, CA: Jossey-Bass, 2005.

Linda Darling-
Hammond
*The Flat World and Education: How America's Commitment to Equity Will Determine Our Future.* New York: Teachers College Press, 2010.

Angeline Stoll
Dillard
*Montessori: The Science Behind the Genius.* New York: Oxford University Press, 2008.

Howard Gardner
*Five Minds for the Future.* Cambridge, MA: Harvard Business School Press, 2009.

Frederick M. Hess *The Same Thing Over and Over: How School Reformers Get Stuck in Yesterday's Ideas.* Cambridge, MA: Harvard University Press, 2010.

Charles M. Payne *So Much Reform, So Little Change: The Persistence of Failure in Urban Schools.* Cambridge, MA: Harvard University Press, 2008.

Daniel H. Pink *A Whole New Mind: Why Right-Brainers Will Rule the Future.* New York: Riverhead Books, 2006.

Peter Sims *Little Bets: How Breakthrough Ideas Emerge from Small Discoveries.* New York: Free Press, 2011.

Douglas Thomas and John Seely Brown *A New Culture of Learning: Cultivating the Imagination for a World of Constant Change*, Seattle, WA: Createspace, 2011.

Bernie Trilling and Charles Fadel *21st Century Skills: Learning for Life in Our Times.* San Francisco, CA: Jossey-Bass, 2009.

Tony Wagner *The Global Achievement Gap: Why Even Our Best Schools Don't Teach the New Survival Skills Our Children Need—And What We Can Do About It.* New York: Basic Books, 2008.

Yong Zhao *Catching Up or Leading the Way: American Education in the Age of Globalization.* Alexandria, VA: ASCD, 2009.

## Periodicals and Internet Sources

Luis A. Albinas and Chris Gabrieli — "Shortchanged by The Bell," *The New York Times*, August 22, 2011.

Steve Denning — "The Single Best Idea for Reforming K–12 Education," *Forbes*, September 1, 2011.

Ellen Gamerman — "What Makes Finnish Kids So Smart?" *Wall Street Journal*, February 29, 2008.

Michael E. Gordon and Oded Palmon — "Spare the Rigor, Spoil the Learning," *Academe Online*, July/August 2010.

Richard H. Hersh — "A Well-Rounded Education for a Flat World," *Educational Leadership*, September 2009.

David L. Kirp — "From Cradle to College," *The Nation*, June 14, 2010.

Arthur E. Levine — "The School of One: The School of Tomorrow," *huffingtonpost.com*, September 16, 2009.

Kathleen Parker — "Our Unprepared Graduates," *Washington Post*, September 30, 2011.

Amanda Paulson — "Why U.S. High School Reform Efforts Aren't Working," *Christian Science Monitor*, January 15, 2010.

Daniel Petter-Lipstein — "Superwoman Was Already Here," *un-schooled.net*, February 23, 2011.

Marilyn Price-Mitchell
"Will Small-Part Fixes Save Public Schools?" *Psychology Today*, September 22, 2011.

Libby Quaid and Donna Blankinship
"The Influence Game: Bill Gates Pushes Education Reform," *USA Today*, October 29, 2009.

Amanda Ripley
"Brilliance in a Box: What Do the Best Classrooms in the World Look Like?" *slate.com*, October 20, 2010.

William C. Symonds
"Pathways to Prosperity: Preparing Workers for the Jobs of the 21$^{st}$ Century," *Harvard Graduate School of Education*, February 2011.

Evan Thomas and Pat Wingert
"Why We Must Fire Bad Teachers," *Newsweek*, March 5, 2010.

Dennis Van Roekel
"In Education, Poor Investment Yields Poor Returns," *Miami Herald*, September 23, 2011.

Vivek Wadhwa
"U.S. Schools Are Still Ahead—Way Ahead," *Businessweek*, January 12, 2011.

Kayla Webley
"Tongue Tied: How Budget Cuts to International Education Will Hurt the U.S." globalspin.blogs.time.com, June 2, 2011.

Marian Wright Edelman
"Getting Children Ready for School," *huffingtonpost.com*, August 12, 2011.

Yong Zhao
"Needed: Global Villagers," *Educational Leadership*, September 2009.

# Index